P9-CAZ-024

# CAREER CHANGE

Stop *HATING* your job, discover what you *REALLY* want to do with your life, and start *DOING* it!

# JOANNA PENN

Copyright © Joanna Penn 2013

First printed in this edition 2013,
updated and rewritten from 2008 print edition. Previously published as
'How to enjoy your job or find a new one'.


The Creative Penn Limited
www.TheCreativePenn.com


The right of Joanna Penn to be identified as the author of this work has been
asserted by her in accordance with the Copyright, Designs and Patents Act,
1988

All rights reserved. No part of this publication may be reproduced, stored in
a retrieval system, or transmitted, in any form, or by any means, electronic,
mechanical, photocopying, recording or otherwise, without the prior
permission of the publishers.

This book is sold subject to the condition that it shall not, by way of trade or
otherwise, be lent, resold, hired out, or otherwise circulated without the
author's prior consent in any form of binding or cover other than that in
which it is published and without a similar condition being imposed on the
subsequent purchaser.

Requests to publish work from this book must be sent to Joanna Penn, care
of The Creative Penn.


ISBN 978-1482046182

Cover: Derek Murphy, Creativindie Book Covers

Interior design: Dean Fetzer at www.GunBoss.com

*For Jonathan, who makes me so happy – your support has enabled me to finally make this transition.*

*And for my Mum, who has always believed in me.*

# CONTENTS

Those who dream by night in the
dusty recesses of their minds wake in the
day to find that it was vanity:
but the dreamers of the day are
dangerous... for they may act their dream
with open eyes, to make it possible."

*T. E. Lawrence, Seven Pillars of Wisdom*

# PREFACE FOR 2012 EDITION

Last New Year's Eve I was at a party with some old University friends. I stood in the corner talking to Kate while the greatest hits of the 80s played on MTV.

"How's work?" she asked. I told her about my latest novel and how my business, The Creative Penn, was going.

"Wow," she said. "You sound so enthusiastic and happy. Your face is just shining."

It was at that point I realized I had finally made the life change I had been working towards for the past four years. Because every other New Year's Eve for the 13 years of my corporate consulting job, I had always changed the subject whenever anyone asked this question. I had never wanted to talk about work because what I did every day wasn't my passion. But this year was different.

I originally wrote this book in 2008 when I was trapped in a corporate job that I hated and couldn't see a way out. I knew that I had to get out somehow and so I wrote this self-help book to try and help myself. I thought that studying how I could improve my situation might also help others, so I put the information into this little book.

At the time, I had no idea how following my own advice might actually change things but **it's now May 2012 and I'm a full-time author-entrepreneur**.

I have published two novels that have sold over 35,000 copies. *Pentecost* and *Prophecy* combine my passions for psychology, religion, art history and kick-ass action-adventure novels, and I'm working on more to come. I run my own business, *The Creative Penn*, which helps people to write, publish and market their own books.

I'm an international speaker, running workshops to help other people fulfill their dreams. I sell online multi-media courses which provide the backbone for my online business. TheCreativePenn.com has also been voted one of the Top 10 Blogs for Writers two years running.

**I truly didn't imagine that my life could change like this,** which is why I'm rebooting this little book in 2012.

After I wrote the first version, I followed the steps I had outlined and changed my own life. Perhaps it will also help you to change your life and find the work that is most meaningful for you.

I want you to see that change is possible but that the incremental steps are often tiny. You may not realize how far you can get if you just look at what you achieve in a week or a month. But each step changes something in you. Over years, great things can happen and your life can totally change. Mine has.

> "Most people overestimate what they can accomplish in a year – and underestimate what they can achieve in a decade."
> *Tony Robbins*

I hope you find the book useful, and you can always contact me with any questions:

*Joanna Penn*
*June 2012*

# Introduction

# CALL TO ACTION

**W**ork doesn't just have to be a way to pay the bills.

Work can give you an opportunity to shine and to grow, as well as to make a living. It can develop your self-esteem and fulfillment as an adult, and as a member of society. The world is constantly reinvented by people's work. But so often people are frustrated in their current job and held back by a blinkered view of their capabilities and the possibilities of what they could do.

## Individuals are capable of having brilliant ideas and implementing them.

You can learn new things, develop and grow. You can use your experience to take the initiative and find more fulfillment. You can contribute to others as well as to your own self-development and find meaning in what you do every day. Work takes up a huge proportion of your life and it can also be part of what makes life meaningful.

**Our life's work is part of what defines us,** but for many people that doesn't equate with what they do every day. Many people don't enjoy their jobs and don't know how to change the situation. You may be one of those people …

If so, congratulations.

You have taken the first step in moving towards the day when you will enjoy what you do.

**This book has come from 13 years searching for happiness in my own work.**

I have experienced the highs and lows of starting my own business (more than once!), worked as an IT consultant in large multinationals as well as small boutique consultancies, and volunteered for charities. My search for the right job has taught me about myself as well as my requirements for enjoying work. But it has taken a long time.

Some of the processes along the way have been painful, but important to the journey. As I have retrained, traveled and soul-searched, I have come to realize that there are significant factors that can help us enjoy work now and also move us towards real purpose.

**This book is a not a 'get-rich-quick' scheme or a way to stop work altogether.**

It is about helping you find meaning and happiness in the job you do now, or in the career you would like to have. It's for those who want to make a change for the better. It contains ideas and tips towards a happier and more fulfilling working life, with easy-to-follow diagrams and processes that you can use right now to start making changes.

**This book is a call to action.**

> "Whatever you think you can do,
> or believe you can do, begin it."
>
> *Goethe*

# HOW TO USE THIS BOOK

This book can be read from beginning to end in chapter order, but you can also navigate your own path based on your particular situation.

## Part 1 outlines the problem of workplace unhappiness and how it affects physical and mental health.

If you hate your current job, you are not alone. Some people say that you just have to accept the way work is nowadays, but the statistics on workplace stress, weight gain and depression show that being unhappy in your work might be slowly killing you. In this section you will learn to recognize the signs that things need to change.

## Part 2 focuses on how you can make some immediate changes to enjoy your current situation more.

This section is specifically targeted at the most common problems people have in their jobs. It focuses on self-development to help you through boredom, and to enable you to identify and follow other opportunities. It will show you ways to take control of your stress and use strategies to manage and reduce it.

There are specific chapters for when you are feeling under-rewarded or trapped as well as ideas to help you take control of your finances in order to maximize your choices in life. There are ideas on enhancing your work/life balance by developing new skills and creativity, and re-focusing on areas outside of work.

## Part 3 is designed to help you find out what you really want to do, and move toward that goal.

It is about finding out who you are and what would be best for you. The Career Change Process is an easy-to-follow map for changing your career, and includes ideas on how to implement those changes.

**There are many reasons why people don't enjoy their jobs,** so not all chapters will be relevant to you. To find the most useful chapters, identify the key categories that apply to you in the following list and then select the appropriate chapters.

There is also a free Companion Workbook that you can download from www.TheCreativePenn.com/careerchange . This workbook contains areas for you to write your thoughts and answers to the questions within the book, as well as copies of the key diagrams for you to fill in. There are related exercises in the workbook whenever you see the Workbook icon as follows:

# SO LET'S GET STARTED!

Which of the following statements apply to your situation? Most people will find there are more than one.

## I'm Bored

"My work is boring, repetitive and doesn't challenge or interest me. I count the minutes I have to be there and I'm desperate to leave at the end of the day."

 **Chapter 3: Develop Yourself**

## I'm Stressed

"My job is too stressful. I have too much work/too little time/too much travel/ not enough holiday/not enough time for relationships/family and no time for the rest of my life. I am overworked, exhausted and heading for burnout or a breakdown."

 **Chapter 4: Coping with stress at work**

## I'm Under-rewarded

"I'm not paid enough, not rewarded fairly for my work, and not recognized for the job that I do."

 **Chapter 5: Being valued and appreciated**

## I'm Trapped

"I feel trapped in this job. I need the money to pay the bills. I'm not qualified for anything else, or I won't get paid so much if I go elsewhere. People depend on me so I have to keep this job."

 **Chapter 6: Escaping the trap**

## I'm Mismatched

"There is a mismatch between what I want to do and what I'm actually doing. I don't know exactly what I want, but I know it's not this. There's no meaning in my job. I feel the work itself is pointless."

 **Chapter 10: What do you really want to do?**

# Part 1:
# "I hate my job"

# CHAPTER 1. IDENTIFYING THE PROBLEM

"In the middle of the road of my life I awoke in a dark wood where the true way was wholly lost."

*Dante Alighieri*

Many of you reading this book will work for 5-6 days per week, for between 8–10 hours a day; some more, some less. This is approximately 40–60 hours per week, and many people work far more. Add on a commute and the occasional weekend you may be asked to help out, or the second job, and you will find that you spend the majority of your waking life working.

I have been an office worker for 13 years, in different companies across Europe, America and Asia Pacific, and this fact seems to be the same everywhere: **most people do not enjoy their jobs.**

The sad thing is that many people may *never* enjoy their jobs if they don't actively start moving towards what they want.

You are reading this book because you feel the same. There may be certain aspects of y-our job that you enjoy – the people, the perks, the salary – **but mainly it is something you have to do in order to fund the rest of your life.**

For so many in our generation, work has become something that has to be done, rather than something to look forward to.

This can leave people feeling trapped. Everyone wants to work at something that is meaningful, that utilizes their skills and is appropriately rewarding. In general, people don't want to stop working completely, but they want to stop working at their particular job. They may not know what to do about it or how to change the situation. The big question they ask is: How do I find the right job for me?

Many people focus on being happy 'sometime in the future' when they earn more money, or when they retire. **But what is the point of waiting that long and living life being miserable now?**

This book stems from working in the city every day like so many millions of others. I used to commute for nearly two hours a day between the central city and the suburbs. Commuter trains and buses are the same all over the world. They are packed with the miserable faces of people going to jobs because *they have to* in order to pay the bills. People have closed expressions and hide behind books or thumping iPods, trying to imagine being somewhere else, and counting the days until the weekend.

I worked in an office and spent most of the day on the computer. I had a quick lunch, often at my desk. I needed a sugar fix at around 3pm and took too many headache pills for the pain that never seemed to go away. I still drink too much coffee. I went home exhausted to dinner, TV and bed, feeling guilty about not making it to the gym again. The exhaustion was mental and yet real enough to prevent me from getting out to exercise.

**Do you recognize this situation?**

> *"Work, paradoxically, does not ask enough of us, yet exhausts the narrow parts of us we do bring to its door."*
>
> *David Whyte, The Heart Aroused*

(w) **What is your working situation like right now?**

What are the particular problems that you want to address?

If you understand what I am talking about, you will know the enormous sense of relief when the weekend comes around, and the looming dread on a Sunday night at the thought of another working week. With the brief high of the pay check, you can reward yourself, then the money is gone again and you must go back to work. This is the reality for most people.

## Is this slavery to the working week slowly killing you?

People are in danger of arriving at retirement in ill health wondering what they have achieved in a lifetime of work.

This is exactly what is wrong with my life. Traveling home in the dark after a long day at work, I feel I haven't achieved much, but no-one notices anyway. I have a stress headache and my neck hurts from my bad desk posture. I am tired even though I have done nothing physically active all day. I don't have the energy to go to the gym now. I just want to go home, have dinner and watch TV. Looking around, I know I'm not the only one on the train feeling like this.

*Joanna Penn, Diaries*

**Can you identify with this?**

## Do you feel as if you have been doing something you don't like for far too long?

Don't worry.

If you feel like this right now, you are not alone.

A multitude of surveys and statistics indicate how many people don't enjoy their jobs. Here are just some of the studies:

"**Approximately 60% of today's workers and 50% of middle managers are unhappy in their current jobs.**" *(Source: Accenture)*

"**Only 29% of Australians polled said they were happy in their jobs**. The number one cause of unhappiness is stress." *(Source: Seek.com.au)*

"**A quarter of workers in Britain are disillusioned with their jobs.** One in three Londoners are trapped in jobs they hate." *(Source: YouGov.com)*

**"Americans hate their jobs more than ever** before in the past 20 years, with fewer than half saying they are satisfied. The trend is strongest among workers under the age of 25, with less than 39% satisfied with their jobs. Overall, dissatisfaction has spread among all workers, regardless of age, income or residence." *(Source: Live Science)*

**"Some surveys have found that 87% of Americans don't like their jobs.** About a million people a day phone in sick. It costs the nation an estimated $150 billion per year in treatment for stress-related problems, absenteeism, reduced productivity and employee turnover." *(Source: Forbes)*

If you feel part of these statistics, isn't it time to rethink the way you work?

There is a huge problem, but you can only solve it for yourself.

# CHAPTER 2. THE RESULTS OF AN UNHAPPY WORKPLACE

**U**nhappiness is a feeling that is difficult to quantify and measure, but the results can be seen in workplace stress, weight gain and depression. These are growing problems for the developed world and now receive a great deal of media attention. You may feel that these terms are too extreme to apply to you, but think of them as a continuum on which everybody sits somewhere.

**Mark where you feel you are on the continuums below and then consider where you want to be.**

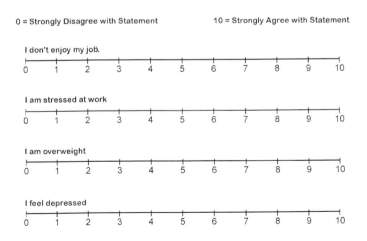

0 = Strongly Disagree with Statement          10 = Strongly Agree with Statement

I don't enjoy my job.

0    1    2    3    4    5    6    7    8    9    10

I am stressed at work

0    1    2    3    4    5    6    7    8    9    10

I am overweight

0    1    2    3    4    5    6    7    8    9    10

I feel depressed

0    1    2    3    4    5    6    7    8    9    10

© The Creative Penn (2008)

## Stress

Some stress is positive. Challenging work brings an edge from the adrenalin of achievement. Unfortunately, most people suffer negative stress (dis-stress) at work, and this is not even considered unusual anymore.

But how do you get the right balance?

Negative stress happens when the job you do is mismatched to what you really want, or when you work long hours at something you don't enjoy, when you have no time to relax and recover. Too much of this pattern can damage your health and your relationships. Many of us have developed a high tolerance or even take a certain pride in this kind of stress without considering the longer-term effects. But stress becomes overwhelming when the ability to cope is outweighed by the number of stressors in your life.

Look at these statistics on negative stress.

**"People's jobs are the single biggest cause of stress** with over a third (36%) of Britons citing it as one of their biggest stressors. 45% of those who have felt stressed have been depressed as a consequence." *(Source: Hazards Magazine)*

"26% of adult Americans reported being on the verge of a serious nervous breakdown." *(Source: American Psychologist)*

**"Workplace stress can double the rate of death from heart disease.** High demands, low control, low job security and few career opportunities contributed to the overall stress measured in the study." *(Source: Centre for the Advancement of Health)*

"Work-related stress (including job insecurity) and fatigue may increase the risk of cold, flu and stomach inflammation.

In one study, employees in demanding jobs developed colds 20% more often than those in less demanding positions." *(Source: Centre for the Advancement of Health)*

"Seven of the top-selling drugs worldwide are either antidepressants or anti-ulcer medications, and stress is cited as a prime factor in the need for both." *(Source: Behavioral Healthcare)*

"Studies show that the greatest number of heart attacks in North America and Western Europe occur between 8am and 9am on a Monday morning." *(Source:Women's Heart Foundation)*

**"Japan has its own word for death from overwork – karoshi.** The major medical causes are heart attack and stroke due to stress. Factors that indicate karoshi are: excessive working hours in a short period, long term excessive work burdens, irregular work hours, infrequent breaks, frequent business trips, shift work, late night work and work-related stress. It is now indicated that Western nations are suffering the same 'disease'." *(Source: Stress.org)*

Stress is now so commonplace in the workplace that a growing industry exists just to manage it. Psychologists investigate it and employers bring in massage therapists, or send people on "mental health" days because of the rising cost of workplace stress. Office workers don't do back-breaking physical work, but many are exhausted by the sheer pace of modern work, the pressure to succeed, or the frustration that comes with the inability to progress.

**Working with certain other people can also generate negative stress.** Many people say that the friends they make at work are the reason to go in every day, but there are also people who can make life at work more stressful. It could be a manager with poor people skills who treats you badly or bullies people, or a co-worker who makes life difficult for everyone. Negative stress from people dynamics can impair thinking, resulting in poor decisions. Social stress can cause people to protect themselves by being hostile or over sensitive.

(W) **What triggers your stress?**

If you know you get stressed but are not aware of what triggers it, try keeping a weekly log. Notice what triggers a stressed feeling and then use the strategies in this book to avoid or manage the situation.

(W) **Go to this diagram in the Workbook**

and add what is stressing you. Circle areas that particularly fit your situation and add your own details.

© The Creative Penn (2008)

## Is stress wearing you down?

Responses to stress have developed from the evolutionary fight/flight mechanism triggered when facing fearful or dangerous situations. When danger is perceived, the body has an immediate stimulant to action, raising the heart rate and releasing hormones to help the body react. This is important if the danger is real and needs an immediate response. In the work environment, negative stress is generated psychologically and may be prolonged. The body's resistance is worn down and the immune system is weakened. If you get sick, the stress is compounded and further undermines the ability to resist new stressors.

High levels of negative stress are associated with high blood pressure, increasing the likelihood of a heart attack or stroke. Stress emotions can cause depression and negativity, also linked with impaired immune function.

**Some physical results of stress** include ulcers, asthma, chronic headaches and migraine, bowel problems and skin disorders. In today's work environment, these physical issues can be compounded by eating badly, not getting enough sleep or exercise, being overweight, or using drugs or alcohol as coping mechanisms.

"I work these 12 hour days, six days a week. Most days I take no lunch, no break. I'm going to end up walking out. I have nothing left to give. It's like someone pounding on your head 11-12 hours a day. For years. Some mornings I wake up, I can't move."

*Sandy, HR Director*
*(Source: Gig: Americans talk about their jobs)*

Sometimes you may not recognize that what you are experiencing is stress-related.

**I have always had headaches that are noticeably worse under stress.** I used to take painkillers several times a day to keep the symptoms at bay. At least twice a month they would flare into migraine and I would have to go home and lie in the dark. I have also had the skin problem of hives, little red spots appearing on the torso. I didn't know what it was and assumed it was just an allergy to something. I went for a massage and the therapist told me how often she saw this on stressed bodies. After I changed my working conditions, the hives went away.

Another friend has Irritable Bowel Syndrome (IBS) which results in chronic abdominal pain and digestive issues. Despite the controls of diet, exercise and medication, it flares up under workplace or emotional stress, which creates a vicious circle of health issues.

## We manifest our stress in our bodies: it can't be compartmentalized.

(w) **Do you have physical symptoms that might be related to stress?**

Workplace stress often means that there is so much going on for you that it is hard to cope with everything at once. You might have a bad day and come home grumpy at your partner or the kids. You stare fixedly at the TV, sink into a glass of wine or eat to feel better. Often it is not one big stressor, but the sheer accumulation of small ones that becomes overwhelming.

## Carry on this way, and you will eventually burn out.

You cannot run on an energy deficit for too long. You will become acutely fatigued, that deep tiredness that can persist for months on end. There's no energy left after work to do anything else, just the need to sleep and recuperate in order to go back to work.

Monitor your burnout symptoms:

- **Physical:** Fatigue, exhaustion, sleep problems, loss of sex drive, headaches, stomach problems

- **Emotional:** Irritability, anxiety, depression, guilt

- **Behavioral:** Aggression, pessimism, defensiveness, cynicism, substance abuse

- **Work related:** Poor performance, absenteeism, being constantly late for work

- **Interpersonal:** Inability to communicate, lack of focus, withdrawal

To further complicate matters, there may be other things as well as work that are causing stress in your life right now.

### Are you dealing with any of these as well as your stress from work?

- Moving house

- Marital difficulties, divorce or break-up of a relationship

- Pregnancy and having a new baby

- Caring for a sick family member

- Death of a parent/ family member/ friend

- Personal illness or chronic pain

Underpinning all of these are the financial concerns bound up with work stress, because for most people, a job is the only form of income.

## ...and what about weight gain?

Office workers lead sedentary lives and yet are often surrounded by food. There are often doughnuts and cookies available in the office kitchens and quick lunches are snatched from food courts. During the days of long meetings, or just hard work it is too easy to have a sugary snack to see you through the afternoon. Or some painkillers with a soda so the sugar and caffeine will see you through the stress headache threatening the afternoon workload.

**Let's face it, sometimes chocolate, chips or soda can be the best part of the working day.** What used to be a treat becomes a daily fix that you deserve because of your hard work and what you have to put up with.

During one particularly stressful year of work, I was living abroad and working ridiculous hours to meet business deadlines. I lived on takeouts and emergency chocolate, and although I went to the gym, I rewarded myself daily for the hard time I was having.

I put on over 20 pounds that year and kept that weight on through the next ten years of work. The coffee and muffin at 10.30, the 3pm sugar fix, the leaving afternoon cake, the drinks after work, the food pleasure for the work pain. I know how the office world works, and I am evidence of how it can affect the waistline.

When the best part of your energy most days is spent at work and you have little time left for exercise, it is clear that commuting and office work are not conducive to a healthy lifestyle. But increasingly, weight gain is tipping into obesity.

The World Health Organization now considers obesity to be an epidemic in the developed world. Modern working life is certainly related to this.

A study has shown that **stress can promote obesity**. A neuro-chemical pathway in the brain promotes fat growth in chronically stressed animals that eat the equivalent of a junk-food diet. *(Source: Washington Post)*

There is a very strong link between job strain (heavy demands, little decision-making power and little social support) and risk of obesity. *(Source: American Journal of Epidemiology)*.

**Nutrition is one of the first things sacrificed to the demands of the job.** Workers say that they skip meals, eat on the run, eat too much junk food and have trouble preparing healthy meals. *(Source: Centre for the Advancement of Health)*

## Feeling depressed?

Stuck in a depressing job, people may feel there is little point in their lives, little joy and little reason to continue trying. Depression can contribute to stress, as stress can contribute to depression. This can feel like a downward spiral.

**"Right now, 1 in 6 workers is experiencing depression, anxiety or stress. That's the elephant in the room."** *(Source: Mind – For better mental health, British Charity)*

**Depression ranks among the top 3 workplace problems** for employee assistance professionals, following only family crisis and stress. *(Source: Mental Health America: Depression in the workplace)*

If you are feeling depressed, remember that you are worth more than just your job and get some professional help.

## So these are some of the problems with modern work.

# "Is the life you're leading worth the price you're paying to live it?"

*Eugene O'Kelly, Chasing Daylight*

People don't like their jobs, they are getting fatter, they are stressed, depressed and it's getting worse every year. It's not a great outlook, so something needs to be done.

It's pretty depressing to read that first section and realize the real effects a difficult work situation can have. But until we really analyze the situation, we can't change our behavior.

(w) **Do you feel that your work life is affecting your health as well as your happiness? What would you like to change about this situation?**

Many of us continue to repeat the same experience, day in, day out, for years, because making a change is too hard. But look at how fast the time flies by. We have this one life and so we have to make the most of it. Too soon, we will be looking back over what we didn't do in our lives.

In *The Top Five Regrets of the Dying*, nurse Bronnie Ware lists the regrets that people have as they transition out of this life.

- **I wish I'd had the courage to live a life true to myself**, not the life others expected of me
- **I wish I hadn't worked so hard**
- I wish I'd had the courage to express my feelings
- I wish I had stayed in contact with my friends
- **I wish that I'd let myself be happier**

Happiness is a choice. Your work life is a choice. **It's not too late to change direction.**

If you're ready… let's begin. Here are some strategies that have made a difference to my working life and which could be used to survive and thrive in yours.

# Part 2:
# How to improve your current situation

# CHAPTER 3. DEVELOP YOURSELF

People frequently don't enjoy their jobs because the work is boring. Everyone enjoys a quiet day, but when the work is not challenging enough, the hours drag by and boredom sets in. There could be too little work to do and you sit there clock watching, or the work itself is repetitive and dulls the mind.

People perform well when given a challenge, the parameters to operate under and then the space to achieve. When people are engaged with the task and committed to it, workplaces become busy and active. When there is a set goal, a time limit and lots to do, people feel they are making a contribution. But many jobs are repetitive and don't stretch people enough, and therefore people slack off.

 **Is your work challenging for you? If not, then analyze why not.**

Did you take the job expecting it to be like this? How long have you been doing it? Have you increased your skill level so that it is now too easy for you?

**One of the most powerful ways to tackle boredom is self-**development, **which may give you the opportunity to move upwards or o**utwards from your current situation. If your problem is boredom, you need to change your situation. Either you need to change your role within your existing company, or find a new job. You may even be able to use some of the time when you are bored at work to focus on self-development.

## Developing yourself as the asset

You do the work and are paid in return. You are your own greatest asset. Therefore, you must focus on self-development and incremental increases in knowledge and skills in order to enhance your value. Continuously improving yourself, both in job-related and other activities will create new opportunities.

> ## "Learning is not compulsory... neither is survival."
>
> ### *W. Edwards Deming*

*"Kaizen"* is a Japanese word that represents self-improvement in incremental amounts. Originally it applied to a manufacturing environment, but it is now used in a broader context as continuous improvement. It is about having an attitude that is always focused on learning and developing.

In the diagram below, John stops learning in school and does not invest in self-development so his learning stays flat throughout adulthood. Jane spends her lifetime looking for opportunities to learn and develop new skills in different areas.

The difference between the two lines is filled with increased opportunities and potential that Jane can take advantage of during her lifetime. These are opportunities that John will never be aware of. Remember: our brain capacity is not fixed. It can be expanded and stretched with new information and stimulation.

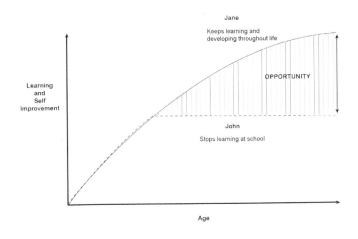

Jane

Keeps learning and
developing throughout life

OPPORTUNITY

Learning
and
Self
Improvement

John

Stops learning at school

Age

© The Creative Penn (2008)

**W** **Plot your own chart in the workbook. Do you feel you have continued learning since school? What are some of the ways in which you have improved your learning and development?**

"Formal education will earn you a living.
Self-education will earn you a fortune."

*Jim Rohn*

There are many opportunities for continuous development and self-improvement. Here are just some examples.

- Apply for company training and corporate programs as most companies have a training budget. You can sometimes even justify spending company training budget on a personal development program if you can demonstrate the benefit. You may be surprised what is on offer if you ask. Some companies have courses that are eligible for college credits, so start by looking within your own workplace for possibilities. If you do workplace training, you can also become more valuable to your employer and are therefore able to bargain for different opportunities, more flexible work time or higher pay. You are proving yourself valuable and they won't want to lose you.

- Many companies run internal training sessions on many different work-related topics. Take advantage of any your workplace offers. Ask your HR manager what development opportunities are available. Become a First Aider, or take some computer skills training in order to add to your experience, and remember to add it to your resume. You never know who you will meet or how this could develop. This kind of networking can open up unexpected opportunities.

- Turn off the TV and read. Watch TED videos, which are short and brilliantly inspiring. This will get you thinking about different things. Consumer TV prevents this kind of thinking because you don't need to use your imagination if you can see it all in front of you. Audios are another way of learning. You can download audiobooks online at Audible.com for a similar price to a physical book, or listen to free podcasts. Use your commuting time to read/listen. Take notes on anything you want to remember.

- Investigate correspondence courses or the Open University. There are now thousands of courses online that you can use to add to your portfolio of knowledge. These don't have to be in your area of work; they can be purely for your own enjoyment and development. These can be done slowly and from a distance, and many have no exams. Payment is usually by module so it can be very affordable.

- Have a look at some Internet courses. iTunes University has courses from Oxford, Yale, Stanford and more available for free in podcast and video format. The Khan Academy has thousands of video tutorials for free. Education is freely available in the world and empowers people to understand and achieve more. I have personally changed my career by taking online courses in blogging and internet marketing, as well as how to write fiction. You don't need another degree to change your direction, because the opportunities to learn are everywhere.

- Take an evening class in a subject you are interested in. There may be free or cheap community classes in various academic subjects as well as different vocational classes. There are classes at hardware stores on DIY skills, so there is something for everyone. The aim is to refresh and expand your mind and increase your skills and confidence.

- Subscribe to websites for information you are interested in. Many websites will send you free updates or eBooks. Sign up for Google Alerts on a chosen subject. I use Google Reader to keep tabs on hundreds of blogs in areas I am interested in.

## "You are the same today as you'll be in five year except for two things: the books you read and the people you meet."

### *Charlie James*

This might sound exhausting to add to your current schedule but you can survive in your current job by keeping your mind and soul alive through learning. It needs determination and motivation when you are exhausted, but record everything you do as an achievement and you will see the effects over time.

**If you improve through any kind of learning, you will boost your self-esteem, open up new possibilities, and meet new people in the process.**

Continuous improvement builds your self-confidence and your experience. It allows you to see beyond your current situation, so that when opportunities come your way, you will be ready to take them.

> (w) **What areas are you interested in developing?**

What are some of the ways you could develop yourself further?

**So, if you are bored at work, you have two choices.**

Stick at what you are doing and just survive, or leverage yourself out of there by developing yourself.

**"We cannot become who we need to be by remaining who we are. Invent yourself every day."**

*Anonymous*

# CHAPTER 4. COPING WITH STRESS AT WORK

Finding positive ways to manage stress will provide a protective buffer so you can cope with stressful situations. The 'stress buffer' can provide a cushion around you, protecting you from being overwhelmed. It won't stop stress happening, but it will enable you to survive.

## No-one is going to change this for you so you need to find ways to deal with your stress.

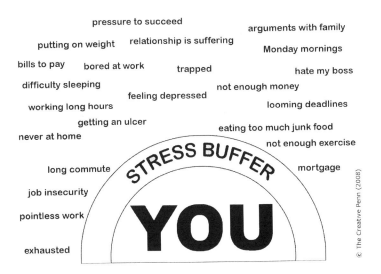

(w) **Here are some ways to build your Stress Buffer. Download the FREE Companion Workbook and write your answers to these questions in this section.**

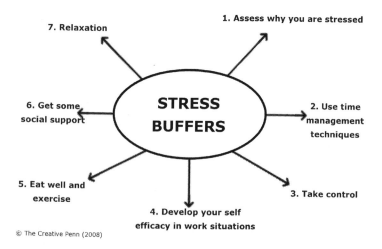

© The Creative Penn (2008)

## 1. Assess why you are stressed

(w) **What are the situations in which you get stressed? Who makes you feel stressed?**

Here are some examples of workplace stress to help you identify your stressors.

- Trying to do a job that doesn't match your values or skills

- Conflict with other people

- Working long hours which leaves you so tired you can't function at home or do things you enjoy

- Not having enough time to do a quality job and then being criticized for under-performing

- No time to learn the skill before being asked to perform it

- Lack of support from other team members who may not even be doing their own jobs properly

There are many more things in the workplace that are stressful. Write down the things that particularly affect you.

## 2. Use time management techniques

You might feel stressed because you don't have the time to do everything that you need or want to do. The key is to actively manage the situation and bring it under your control. Try the following time management techniques.

- Write down everything you have to achieve and by when. Even the small things add up. Having a list immediately gives you more control. I am a chronic list maker. I just use bits of scrap paper that I delight in throwing away every day as I cross off some things and then make the list for the next day. You don't need apps and tools, just a pen and paper is a great start. The simpler, the better.

- Estimate how long these things will take and rate them in terms of urgency and importance. Although this list will keep changing, sometimes it is necessary to write it all down so you can get some perspective. It may also be useful to have a record of what you actually do in your job to convince a Team Leader that you have too much work for anyone to handle in the time available.

- Review your work related items with your manager so they are aware of the competing demands on your time. You can even ask for more help if necessary. You may find that they are unaware of your workload and there may be others who can help you with it. Managers prefer to know in advance if deadlines will be missed.

- Start booking people into time slots in your calendar to keep them from turning up at your desk with impromptu requests.

- Start saying 'No' when people ask you to do things outside the boundary of your prescribed job. This may be very difficult for some people who want to be helpful all the time, but it is essential if you are to be less stressed.

- Some workplaces have "no meeting days" or only have meetings in the mornings, so people also have time to achieve their actions by the next meeting. You could suggest this for your workplace or your team.

- Use your diary to block out time for specific activities that aren't work related. I still use this technique, and have an old Filofax paper diary that I use with multi-colored pens to control my time. I split my time now between writing fiction and doing more structured tasks for my business, including preparation for speaking and courses. I plan my time weeks in advance with time slots of fiction/creativity and slots for the rest. If you don't plan it, time runs away from you.

- Only read your email after 12 noon every day, or at least 10am. You could also try allocating specific periods of time for email, rather than constantly checking it. This will give you quality time to actually get things done.

- Work away from your desk in a meeting room, or work from home if you can to get admin-heavy work completed

**(w)** In what ways could you implement time management techniques to make your work life less stressful?

## 3. Take control

If you blame your stress on aspects of your life which are not under your influence, you will not be able to reduce or control your stress.

## Take ownership of what is stressing you.

If you acknowledge that you have control over what stresses you, you can deal with it by actively solving the problem. If you believe it is someone else's fault or responsibility, then nothing will change.

## Own it, change it.

> "Emancipate yourselves from mental slavery. None but ourselves can free our minds."
>
> *Bob Marley, Redemption Song*

## 4. Develop your self-efficacy

Self-efficacy is your belief in your own capability to do something. It may be a proven capability based on something you have achieved or it may be the belief that you can do a new thing given the opportunity.

If you believe you can do something, you will feel more in control and therefore less stressed. If you try something new and it works, you will feel you have achieved. You will have increased your self-efficacy. If it doesn't work, then you can learn from it and the lesson will also improve your self-efficacy. **It is all about how you perceive the situation.**

For example, I started three businesses before The Creative Penn. Each of the previous businesses 'failed' within a year after much hard work and money spent. As much as the experiences were painful, I learnt a great deal each time that enabled me to go on to later success. I perceived that the failures increased my abilities to eventually run a successful business, so my self-efficacy improved even though I 'failed.'

## "If you want to succeed, double your failure rate."
### *Thomas Watson, founder of IBM*

Your comfort zone is where you are happy doing your work or using your abilities. Part of developing self-efficacy is to stretch your comfort zone and increase your skill level so you can function without being stressed in the outer limits.

## If you don't challenge yourself, you will never know what you are capable of.

Here are some ways to improve your self-efficacy.

**Identify what you have achieved** – at work or in other areas of your life. Make a detailed record of your successes and acknowledge that you have skills, and that you are valuable.

**Identify where your comfort zone is.** Where are the boundaries of your skills? Where do you lose your self-confidence? For example, you may be happy speaking in front of colleagues at a staff meeting, but not at a conference of 500 people.

**Find ways to apply your skills** to the boundaries of your comfort zone in order to extend it out further.

**List ways you could improve** in a specific area by developing new skills.

Aim to **put yourself in a new situation** in a manageable way in order to increase your comfort zone without becoming too stressed.

Once you have tackled a new situation, add it to the list of what you have achieved and learned. **Celebrate another step forward!**

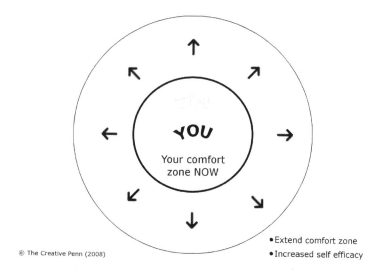

© The Creative Penn (2008)

- Extend comfort zone
- Increased self efficacy

(W) **Fill the diagram with the areas that are in your comfort zone now, and areas where you would like to extend it. What will you actually do to extend these areas?**

Self-efficacy can be improved by doing things that push the boundaries of what you think you can achieve. For me, this has involved physical challenges at several key life stages.

When I was 15, I went on an outdoor adventure course in England where we spent a week hiking and doing activities that were often challenging mentally and physically. It was a life-shaping time and helped me at a time when we are all vulnerable, moving into the adult world.

At age 30, I had just finalized my divorce and I was going through a different kind of transition. I decided to go on an Outward Bound adventure for 7 days in the wilds of New Zealand's South Island. It was another challenging time that pushed me past my limits to collapse. But I also rediscovered some things about myself. We can find truth in the hard moments, but it is up to us to seek them.

## 5. Eat well and exercise

Everyone knows about the benefits of a proper diet and exercise, but so often other priorities get in the way. Chapter 2 outlined some of the ways in which the modern workplace affects our health.

 **Revisit your stress diagram. Are any of your current physical problems related to stress?**

Eating nutritious food boosts the immune system and modulates your emotional state. Exercise increases healthy blood flow to the brain and releases endorphins which make you feel good. It also gives you time to think away from the work situation. You can listen to your favorite music and change how you feel whilst exercising. You can burn off your frustration by running or swimming. Physically stretching yourself can quiet the mind and enable you to sleep well.

Exercise improves self-esteem, and makes you feel you are actually doing something to manage your stress, as opposed to doing nothing. You may not feel like it, but if you can get out of the door and do some exercise, you will feel much better for it and it will reduce your stress levels. Diarize it, and get it done.

## 6. Social support

Social support may be time with your partner, friends or professionals who can support you through difficult times. It is incredibly important to have supportive people in your life when you are dealing with stress. Many workplaces now offer direct counseling services or phone lines where you can talk about what is going on anonymously. Sometimes just talking about a problem with a professional can help.

However, don't dwell on your stress for too long. You get what you focus on, and if you focus on the negatives over time, they will not change. So use your friends for support, and be there for them in return, but make sure you have a plan to get out of that situation.

(w) **Who acts as your support at the moment?**
**Who do you support in return?**
**Would you benefit from seeing a professional?**

## 7. Relaxation

Relaxation helps prevent and control the overwhelming panic that can occur when you are stressed. You must give your mind and body some time off. It doesn't have to cost you anything, but you do need to commit some time for relaxation. Again, diarize it and make it happen.

I am definitely guilty of not making relaxation a priority. My husband says I am like "a Ferrari without a fuel gauge" in that I try to do everything fast and then run out of fuel and collapse in burnout mode. Learning how to relax is a lesson I keep returning to.

Here are some suggestions based on my experiences:

- Sleep more. Your mind is powerful and can work on problems when you are asleep. As well as feeling refreshed when you wake up, you may also have the answers to some of your problems. If you can sort out any sleep issues you have, you may find other things also resolve. I sleep in an eye mask and ear plugs now to make sure I am in silence and darkness. If I have a bad day, the best thing to do is go to bed, because things are often better the next morning. We know when children are overtired, because they are grumpy or emotional, so why don't we recognize that in ourselves?

- Turn off the TV. Be silent or read a book. Stop watching or reading the news obsessively. TV is designed to capture our attention and spike our adrenalin with fear and worry. If you disconnect from constant media, you will find the space to relax. Take the TV out of the bedroom so you aren't tempted to stay awake too long.

- Listen to some relaxation or meditation CDs. These are often available in your local library if you don't want to buy any.

- Learn a relaxation technique like meditation, progressive muscle relaxation or visualization. After many years of trying different techniques, now I just set the timer for 10 minutes and sit and breathe, concentrating on my breath as it enters and leaves my body. I can do more time if I want to, but 10 minutes is such a short length of time that there is no excuse to miss it. It has also shown me that I tend to hold my breath when I am stressed. Try being mindful about your body.

- Have a regular massage. Ask the therapist where you hold your stress in your body. This knowledge can help you identify which physical areas to focus on relaxing.

- Take a yoga class. Breathe and stretch more. I used to find yoga a challenge until I learned that it wasn't a competition. Just let your body be in the moment, relax into it and be gentle on yourself. There is no judgment in yoga, just practice.

- Get a hammock and spend some quality time in it. There is something inherently relaxing about being in a hammock. I guarantee you will fall asleep in one. You can get a stand instead of using hooks which can be more practical inside a home.

- See a professional hypnotist for relaxation and de-stressing.

- Laugh. Get some funny movies. Go to a fun park and go on the rides. Be silly.

- Get out into nature and walk. Go and look at something that is not the city.

- Just STOP. Allocate time to just lie on the couch for hours with a book. I find the Kindle to be a great device for relaxation time. You don't even have to get up to get a new book. Is your To Do list really as important as letting your body and mind rest? Don't do anything. You are allowed. You have permission.

## "I find myself being mentored by the land once again. I too can bring my breath down to dwell in a deeper place where my blood soul restores to my body what society has drained and dredged away."

### *Terry Tempest-Williams*

Manage your stress by relaxing regularly. You will find that the sense of calm spills into your daily life.

(W) **Which of these techniques do you think could help you? What three steps could you take right now to incorporate any of them into your life?**

# CHAPTER 5. BEING VALUED AND APPRECIATED

"A fair day's pay for a fair day's work" is fair enough. However, a lot of the time you go the extra mile and work the long hours. **A word of praise, a personalized email of encouragement or thanks, can make all the difference to how you feel about a situation.**

These mementos last longer than the pay check and show that someone has valued what you have done. There are some managers and even companies people love to work for because they are known for having a special way of treating people.

I have had a couple of managers who helped me change my life through their attitude to flexible working and who rewarded employees with written and spoken praise. But in my experience, they are rare stars in a bleak corporate world. These managers recognize that people really are their means of doing exceptional business, and treat them accordingly. However, too often it seems people are treated as resources rather than individuals valued for their own sake.

So why is this important? Isn't it enough that we get paid for our work?

For many people in the Western world, the pay is well above the poverty level. Work is generally not just about survival anymore. Once basic needs are fulfilled, then work must ideally be about something more than that.

People want the opportunity to develop and grow, and

something other than just financial gain. To motivate people, there must be personal growth, something that can be achieved, a goal to reach towards, respect from others and rewards appropriate to the situation. Self-esteem is also affected by what peers and managers think of you, as well as how much you perceive you are valued.

## What kind of work will make you feel valued?

The following areas contribute, in part, to making work more positive and demonstrating that people are valued.

Trusted to do the job without micromanagement

Appropriately rewarded

Respected as a person

Appreciated

Contributing to other people or the environment

Opportunity and encouragement

Responsibility and trust

Challenge that stretches but does not stress

© The Creative Penn (2008)

- Self-management and autonomy. Being trusted to do the job without micro-management.

- Helping others. Doing things for other people can help us escape negativity, especially if our jobs seem pointless or repetitive. In being needed by others, individuals can feel useful and valued.

- Being able to make informed decisions and not have those decisions overturned.

- Taking control and responsibility over specific areas of work.

- The ability to achieve goals and succeed at tasks.

- Being given the opportunity and encouragement to take the initiative and act creatively without fear of blame.

- Being rewarded appropriately and in proportion to the job done.

- Confidence in being able to plan personal life around work. Stability in working hours.

- Being treated well and respected as a person and not as just a company resource. Acknowledgement of other important roles such as partner or parent.

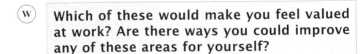

**(W) Which of these would make you feel valued at work? Are there ways you could improve any of these areas for yourself?**

## Gratitude as an extension of being valued

Gratitude can sometimes seem in short supply in the workplace, but thanking people helps at every level of the organization. Gratitude focuses the mind on the positives in your life. Whatever your situation, you can find a great deal to be thankful for.

**It is important to be grateful about where you are now, in order to be grateful about where you are going.**

Even if you don't enjoy your job, you can be grateful for the income it brings you, the experiences you can have, the friends you make and for the opportunities that are just around the corner.

You might be thinking, "no one thanks me, no one appreciates me". But if you give out positive energy and appreciation, you will find it coming back to you. Start appreciating what other people do at work. Focus on the positives, rather than the negatives. Try thanking other people, and they will begin to appreciate you in return.

**Say thank you more often.**

Try saying "Thank you" on your daily commute, as this will give you a regular time every working day when you can reset your mind to the positive. Take several minutes each day to find things for which to say thank you. It doesn't matter who you say thank you to – God, the Universe, or other people. You can say these in your head, or out loud, or write them in a journal – whichever feels best for you.

 **What do you have in your life to be thankful for?**

This daily practice of gratitude puts the mind into a positive state for the day and will stop that feeling of dread as you travel to work. It may also stop you from being grumpy when you get home. Start with one or two things – your health, your family –

and you will soon get the hang of it and find other things to be grateful for. Also, be thankful for the opportunities that are on their way to you, the people you will meet who will help you, and the ideas that come to you about your future.

Saying thank you to people for doing their jobs well is important. No matter what the job is, people need appreciation. It shows respect for that person and makes them feel more valued. You are likely to be treated better in return. Saying thank you is also a way to help difficult situations. For example, someone has made a critical comment about your work. Take a deep breath and then say "Thank you for your feedback – I appreciate the time you have put into it." This can alter the dynamics of the situation in such a way that the criticism loses its sting and you can have an honest conversation about the subject.

Being grateful in advance can also boost your confidence. If you can be thankful for achieving something, even before you have achieved it, then you are more likely to believe that you can reach that goal. Whenever I speak in public, I spend ten minutes beforehand writing down how grateful I am for the opportunity and for all the ways the talk will touch people. It helps me focus on how I can help the audience, rather than on how I am feeling. I used to do a similar exercise before job interviews, or any situation where I wanted a specific outcome. Whatever happened, it made me feel more in control.

So think about the type of job you really want and how that will make you feel valued, and then be grateful that the job is coming to you. Focus on what you want, not what you don't want.

# "What you think about, and thank about, you bring about."

## *Dr John de Martini*

# CHAPTER 6. ESCAPING THE TRAP

These are the most common reasons people feel trapped in their jobs.

## Money

The job brings in the money needed for the rest of life. It gives us income security and may be within an industry that pays well. When people are qualified for a job they are paid more than for a job they are new at. Starting at the bottom again means less income so it is hard to move on easily. Escaping the money trap will be covered in detail in Chapter 7.

## Status

If people have a certain status based on how much they earn, or the job they do, they may also feel trapped by the need to live up to what other people think of them. For example, when I left a highly paid and well respected job as an IT consultant to become a full-time author-entrepreneur, it not only affected my income but also my status and self-esteem. It was hard to face the changes in attitude that people had towards me, and there was definitely a time when I wanted to run back to the safety of the old ways. So this is a trap I know well.

## Perception

Sometimes people are trapped by their own ideas about the opportunities they have and they don't know how to get out of their current situation. They perceive that there are no other options for them other than to stick with the job they are in.

(w)

> **Do you feel trapped in your job? What are you trapped by?**

## The theory of 'learned helplessness'

Psychologist Martin Seligman talks about the theory of learned helplessness, which explains how people become trapped in situations that they feel they can't get out of.

When life is painful or difficult and people learn to live with their problems for a long time, it is difficult to see a way out, even when the door is open. The more you allow situations to be in control of you, the less you are able to see opportunities or break out. It is important to challenge this cycle of thinking and change your perception of what is around you so you can escape this 'learned helplessness.'

**The truth is: what you perceive is just a tiny piece of reality.**

There are unlimited possibilities. You just need to break down the mental barrier that stops you seeing them. The picture below illustrates how you can become stuck in your own perceived situation, but if you can just break down the walls, you will see there is a different reality out there. It just takes a mind shift.

# Actual Reality

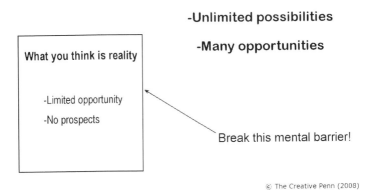

-Unlimited possibilities

-Many opportunities

What you think is reality

-Limited opportunity

-No prospects

Break this mental barrier!

© The Creative Penn (2008)

The brain processes a great deal of information from the world around. In general people are unconscious of most of it. We have to be, otherwise it would overwhelm our senses and we couldn't function normally.

**What is perceived consciously is controlled by your personal filters. These are developed over time based on past experiences and expectations.** The filters construct the wall around your world, and it can be hard to see beyond what they enclose.

If you are trapped in a certain way of seeing yourself and your situation, your brain filters will only allow that type of information to be processed and you will not see the means to your escape.

If you think that this job is the only one you can get, it will be the only one available to you.

If you believe you are trapped, then you are.

**But there are opportunities: you just need to see them and the way will be opened for you.**

**(w)** **What are some of the thoughts that control your situation?**

Are there ways you could change your thinking to alter how you see the world? How can you break those mental barriers?

> "Sometimes we stare so long
> at a door that is closing,
> that we see too late the one that is open."
>
> *Alexander Graham Bell,*
> *Inventor of the telephone*

## Expectations of others

Your opinion of yourself is often based on what other people think and expect of you. This can relate to the job you do, your age, your perceived class in society, your friends, and how you define yourself.

Individuals are expected to have a job that earns a steady wage, and to be achieving something. Parents expect you to earn enough to support yourself. Schools expect you to go to College/University or get a 'proper' job. Jobs expect you to be promoted. We have all been measured in tests since starting school and this competition and measurement continues into the work situation. All of this permeates into our behavior and view of ourselves over time.

**It is easy to end up imprisoning yourself with what you think is appropriate for someone in your position.** You decide you want to be viewed in a particular way, and then you behave in a way to back that up.

For example, when I worked as an IT consultant in London, I had an 'appropriate' car for my status, even though it was costing me far more than I could afford. I also behaved in ways that I believed were expected of my job title and level of earnings. Over time, I became increasingly uncomfortable with this and eventually I needed to escape. I had built my own behavioral cage and to break out of it I had to make some radical changes. For me, that meant leaving the job and in fact, the country, to break out of an established pattern.

You can see that perceived status is a powerful thing!

 **Are you trapped in your job because it is part of what is expected of you? Are you behaving in ways that are expected but do not fit with what you really want?**

## Escaping the trap

First, you need to look at what your current reality is.

Are you constrained by your own thoughts and expectations?

If so, read Chapter 3 and start developing yourself so that new opportunities open up. Learn more about yourself, about money and work possibilities and your situation will start to change.

If you are trapped by status or the desire to fulfill how others see you, then you have a choice. Continue with the job and find other ways to enjoy your life (Part 2), or to change your job to free yourself (Part 3).

 **What will you do to get out of the trap?**

# CHAPTER 7. MAKING MONEY...
# AND KEEPING HOLD OF IT

Some people feel unrewarded financially for the job they do. Others may be paid enough, but are a slave to the pay day. This chapter will cover some important financial concepts, offering practical tips for how to make the most of your money in order to give yourself more choices.

> ## "Most people work just hard enough not to get fired and get paid just enough money not to quit."
>
> ### *George Carlin*

**This is an emotional topic** and I struggle with this as much as anyone. Even though I have earned an excellent wage as a consultant over the years, I let inexperience and bad money management stop me from escaping the trap sooner. I have made investments that didn't work and bought things that were costly and pointless. I have been struck by 'shiny object syndrome' and tried following the latest 'get rich quick' trends. I also entered into property investing just before the global financial crisis. But I have continued to study and learn.

We all make mistakes and then we learn from them. In this chapter, I share some of my own personal realizations as well as wisdom from far more knowledgeable people.

## Escaping the money trap!

Many people would say that they have to do their job for the money, and that spending at the weekend is part of the reward. But often we spend too much, and it can become a cycle of being trapped into waiting for the next pay check. Once people are trapped financially, it becomes difficult to break out of this cycle.

Few people are financially educated or spend much time planning their financial future.

Most were not taught in school about how to budget, fill in a tax return, and look at investing or how to measure and improve our personal wealth. Our education system also conditions students into a certain way of thinking about earning money, working at a job and receiving a pay check. But with state pensions practically non-existent, healthcare under question, and jobs uncertain, we all need to consider our financial options, now and for the future.

This pattern of earn-spend remains throughout life, unless time is consciously spent understanding about how money works and becoming financially educated. It is not enough to work for the present and spend today, not thinking too far into the future or planning for retirement.

Yes, everyone has to spend. There are bills to pay and everyone needs to eat as well as pay the rent/mortgage. Plus we need to have fun!

But there are choices we can make that can get us out of this never-ending cycle, or at least give us some breathing space.

 **Do you see yourself in this cycle? How does it make you feel right now?**

## How can you make the most of the money you earn?

You earn money in your job: the trick is to keep hold of some of it. If you implement some of these strategies, you will give yourself more choices about the work that you do and the life you lead.

**If you take action to control your money, you will find more opportunity to enjoy your life and your job.**

You can invest in self-development, perhaps towards a different career altogether. If you have some extra money, you can pay off some debt so you don't feel trapped where you are now. You can create a safety net or buffer to give you a chance to start something new. You will feel there is hope in your future that you will make it out of the situation you are in now.

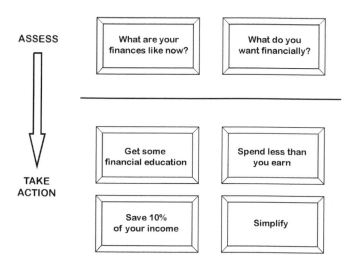

© The Creative Penn (2008)

Here are some initial steps.

## Assess: What are your finances like now?

Be honest. You are only trying to fool yourself if you exaggerate any of the figures or reduce your debt levels in your assessment.

(W)    **Give yourself a financial health-check.**

- How many days/weeks could you live with your present lifestyle if you had to stop work tomorrow?

- How much have you saved for emergencies?

- What is the value of your assets? (what do you own e.g. house, car, investments)

- How much is your total debt? (what you owe other people e.g. mortgage, personal loan, car finance, student loan, credit card debt)

- What are you worth? (total assets minus total debt)

- How much do you have saved for your retirement?

- What is your income every month?

- Are you dependent on your job, your spouse, or the government for this income? Where does your income come from?

- What are your expenses every month? (Fixed outgoings like rent, utilities, food, travel as well as variable expenses like entertainment or clothes)

- What are you left with every month? (income minus expenses)

- What are you putting away for your retirement? How are you investing right now?

## Assess: What do you want financially?

People don't usually think too much about what they want financially because it seems obvious. We all want enough money to fund our lifestyles and buy the things we want. We want to be able to pay the bills, educate the children, keep the family happy and have a holiday every year.

But think ahead a little. Have you ever written down what you want financially for the rest of your life?

- What do you want your life to be like in the future? Or even, as soon as possible!

- How much money will you need to live that life? Is it possible with your current income?

## Get some financial education

**You need to know the financial basics** to get anywhere. If you don't know what 'assets' and 'liabilities' are or if you only have a vague sense of the possibilities in investments, then you need to get some financial education. Is this boring? Yes, it can be, but it's about your freedom and what is more important than that?

Read some books (there is a list under Resources), see a financial advisor or go to one of the many online sites that offer financial education. I recommend Ramit Sethi's *I will teach you to be rich* as a great starter book and website.

Once you understand how money works and how it can best be used, how you think about your money and how you use it will change.

**Find out about investment options that suit you.** Many people think the jargon around investing keeps them out of the game, but it doesn't take too long before you understand some of the concepts.

It is critical to know yourself, your risk profile and what you enjoy before you leap into an investment. I learned about property investment the hard way. There's no such thing as passive income. You have to work at everything, and to be successful with investing you have to be passionate about learning the best way to do things and actively manage your portfolio. If you want to do some interesting investing, then definitely do your research first. A professional financial planner may be able to help with this.

> (W) **What are some of the questions you have about money and investments? Where could you find the answers?**

## Take Action: Spend less than you earn

This may be basic but so many people don't actually do it!

For example, when you think about how much your salary is, you think of the gross amount (the amount before tax and deductions). If you divide this by 12, you have a monthly figure. But if you take out taxes, deductions like superannuation, insurance and then repayments and regular bills, it may not leave you much left over for the fun stuff. So you need to know what you earn and what you are spending.

Spending money is addictive and a vice everyone enjoys to some extent. You work hard, and as you earn more, you spend more. If you get a raise, you can buy that new car or new clothes, or get a better apartment in a better area.

I was certainly trapped in this cycle as an IT consultant working in large corporates.

Earning a good wage meant that I never had to really worry about what I was spending, so I didn't keep a close eye on it. Even when my income went up, I spent it so there was still nothing left at the end of the month. It was only after several years of this that I actually realized what was happening and changed the way the money flowed.

## Is it possible to do things differently?

**Yes. It is.** Try some of these tactics for taking control of your money back.

**Think before you buy.**

Do you really need this? What does it add to your life right now? Are you buying it because of what you want other people to think, or are you not thinking at all? Will you still want it in six months? If not, is it worth it? It's easier to control your impulse buying if you use cash or a debit card, instead of a credit card. When we moved countries, it was impossible to get a credit card and now we have adjusted to cash purchasing which changes your perspective and makes you think before buying. I also know someone who keeps her credit card in a separate envelope in her bag, wrapped around with elastic bands. The hassle of getting it out provides an extra barrier to using it.

**Analyze your credit card bill or bank statement.**

Go through the paper copy or download it. Categorize and total it based on the expenses, e.g. supermarket shopping, takeaways and restaurants, entertainment etc. Look at how much you spent on things that weren't necessary. How many items on your bill do you not even remember? Are you surprised by how much it adds up to?

**How many of those expenses could you scale back on and how much would it save you per week or per month?**

Cutting back on some things will mean more money available for what is important. For example, taking your own sandwiches every day instead of buying lunch could add up to a plane flight somewhere exciting in just a few months.

## Save 10% of your income

I first read this suggestion in *The Richest Man in Babylon* years ago, but I didn't take action. Ten percent seemed such a small amount at the time that I just didn't do it as it didn't seem worthwhile. I didn't set aside a separate account, but said to myself, "I'll just put some money away when I have some left over at the end of the month." Of course, that never happened! I didn't understand the power of habits. You need to establish a habit, even with tiny steps and then grow from there.

Eventually I started putting an amount away with automated payments when I worked in Australia, where it is mandatory to make a contribution to pension/superannuation of at least 9%, which I increased to 12%.

**The best way to do this is to automate it.**

Some people do this on top of superannuation payments, or tithe 10% to church or charities. However you manage the income, it's best to do it before you even see the residual amount in your bank account. Once it's there, you will spend it. If you haven't paid off your debts yet, then direct the 10% there.

This approach is recommended by so many wealth coaches for the following reasons.

- Discipline with money – You have committed to save, you have taken action and you are mastering this amount of money. As it grows you will have the discipline to carry on saving, so you won't spend it. This proves to yourself that you can control money. It doesn't control you. You are a saver, not a spender. This is important for your mindset about money.

- Attraction for more money – Interest compounding on the account over the years makes the growth accelerate. Compound interest is when interest is paid into the account, which in turn grows the principal, and in turn generates more interest.

- Basis for further investment – As the amount grows you can use some of it for further investment.

- A safety net – Although this account is not meant to be touched, it is a safety net in case of emergency. It is there if you lose your job, or you need surgery, or you are in an accident, or a loved one needs help. Life will throw curve balls at you. Having some money in an account you won't touch unless it is an emergency is important in case you do really need it someday.

**Take action now and open an account for your 10% money.**

Think of it as your discipline, your safety net, your dreams, and your money confidence and watch it grow. Don't spend it on something you think you really want, as chances are you will want something else in six months' time. It's not for spending. It's for your future. If you have the discipline to do this, you will also see a change in your attitude towards money quite quickly.

**What is 10% of your income now? Or even 5%? Will you commit to putting that into a lifetime account? How much will you have in this account after five years?**

## Simplify

Simplifying your life will reduce your expenses and also has the effect of reducing stress and worry. Examples of simplifying include:

- Moving away from the central city and tempting restaurants and bars will result in lower rent/mortgage repayments and less expenditure on entertainment

- Cooking for yourself instead of going to restaurants regularly

- Getting a smaller car resulting in lower fuel costs and a lower car loan if you need one. Or getting rid of the car completely if you live somewhere with adequate public transport.

- Going through your house and establishing what you really need and what you don't use anymore. Have a garage sale or use the internet to sell whatever you don't need. This may mean you can move somewhere smaller.

You may find that simplifying enables you to cut your expenses so much that you need a lower income to live on. You can then use this money to invest or as a safety net to fund your move into doing something you love.

**This simplification is part of how I moved from being an IT consultant to growing my own business.**

My husband and I were living in a four bedroom house in Brisbane, Australia, with all the furniture and 'stuff' that one accumulates to fill such a space. We had a car and the expenses that entailed. In moving back to the UK as part of the transition to being a full-time author-entrepreneur, we downsized to a one bedroom flat and no car. We also rented a fully furnished flat, so we sold all our furniture and gave much of our stuff to charity. We use public transport which is much easier to do in London. Basically, we downsized our life and simplified our financial needs to enable more flexibility in using money for our core needs – rent, food and health – while also meaning we could live on less income, meaning I could give up being a consultant to go full-time on my business.

I also found this de-cluttering to be a liberating experience and **I worry so much less now**. We now have more freedom with less baggage to carry through life. Having a small flat means we are mindful of purchases that take up space. This is one of the reasons I now buy ebooks instead of the thousands of print books I used to hoard. These are active life choices resulting in greater financial freedom and the ability to choose the next steps.

(W) **List the ways that you could possibly simplify your current lifestyle to free up more money. Prioritize the top 5 and start implementing them.**

"Money isn't the most important thing in life, but it's reasonably close to oxygen on the 'gotta have it' scale."

*Zig Ziglar*

# CHAPTER 8. BEING CREATIVE

Many jobs are not inherently creative and are not even meant to be. Learning to be successful at work often means we spend years forcing ourselves into rigid environments. We then lack the energy for creativity out of work. But the lack of creative expression and the dulling of the creative self can be part of why people do not enjoy their work and their life more.

**Creativity is an important part of being human.**

It's not about being a great painter or musician. There are so many aspects to creativity and it can be a doorway to learning new things about yourself. Even if you don't want to change your job to a creative one, you can do things in your spare time that will inspire you.

Many people in offices work with computers that don't allow creative expression. Rules and codes, methodologies, efficiency and repetition are the necessary hallmarks of the office job. Most workers in business use word processors and spreadsheets, accounting packages, inventory systems and point-of-sale systems. Many spend hours each week frustrated at the difficulty in using these programs and don't find the computer a creative tool. Office workers are schooled in business writing, in standard fonts, in corporate marketing brands with no variation from these themes, no way to express individuality other than to use different clip art in the next PowerPoint presentation.

**But interestingly, the changing way we work is also changing the importance of creativity in the workplace.**

Knowledge workers are now more often prized for unique ways of looking at problems, finding creative solutions to business issues and seeing patterns in data. These are the attributes of a mind that is more creative than linear. In some circles, the MFA (Master of Fine Arts) is now considered more important than the ubiquitous MBA. However, this may be true among more enlightened companies, but for many, this knowledge hasn't filtered down to the day-to-day working life of most corporates.

**Humans are innately creative, and repressing this instinct can be self-destructive.**

Everyone had creativity in abundance during childhood when there was little concern with what others thought. As children grow up they are taught to be scared of looking stupid, of what others might say, and how not to stand out from the crowd. Some people think they will get creative again in their retirement, but why wait that long for the joy that creativity can bring you now?

**I spent years in an academic and then corporate environment, squashing my creativity into a little box, scared to express it for fear of ridicule and judgment.** I didn't think it had any place in my very serious life of advancement and achievement. I came to a point where I just didn't believe I had any creativity in me at all. That was for other people, not me. And I think that's when I truly felt I hit rock bottom. If all I was involved in was regurgitating other people's work or writing meaningless corporate documents, then what was the point?

So back in 2007, I started to read self-help books and discovered affirmations. You create a statement that encapsulates what you want to be and then repeat it to yourself. It's a way to change a mindset that then allows you to take steps towards achieving a specific goal. My affirmation was "I am creative, I am an author." I felt neither of those things and I couldn't say it out loud for a while, but I kept repeating it and eventually started saying it out loud. Telling myself "I am creative" somehow released a block in me and enabled me to start creating and exploring.

Fast forward to 2012 and I am creative, I am an author and my business is called The Creative Penn. You can read more about this in my bonus article, *From Affirmation to Reality*, included at the back of the book.

> # "In ordinary life, creativity means making something for the soul out of every experience."
> ## *Thomas Moore*

Finding ways to express yourself inside or outside of work brings greater joy to what you do, because you are enjoying yourself more. You can be creative with basic materials and little money. You don't even have to create things yourself, you can go and look at the results of other people's creativity and at least find some escape there.

## Go find some inspiration

Many people think they aren't creative but often the reason is because their creative well is dry.

**You need to fill yourself up with ideas in order to be creative.**

If there is nothing left inside because you have used it all to survive at work, then don't be surprised if you find it hard to be creative. You need to go and have a look at what is inspirational in the world.

Looking at other people's creations may spark new ideas and refresh your mind. This might be an art exhibition, listening to music, seeing an independent film, going to a garden center, anything to stimulate the mind and creative soul. Even simple things can start the process. When I used to feel crazy at work, I would go to bookshops at lunchtime and browse travel picture books for escapism.

One way to jump start your creativity is to visit a modern art gallery. It might be a lottery in terms of what exhibition is on, but the point is to get out of your mental comfort zone, so go anyway.

(W) **Find a modern art gallery near you and make a date to go there. Write down what you experience there.**

Make up your own mind about what the artwork means. The glorious thing is that it is not usually obvious, or even necessary, to explain what the exhibits mean. Modern art can be confrontational as some pieces will make you uncomfortable, challenge you and make you think. These feelings could be channeled to form the foundation of a new creation of your own. I have found some pieces stick in my mind for years and provide ongoing inspiration for warped creativity. Look at Patricia Piccinini or Ron Mueck's sculptures and you'll know what I mean.

### Sydney, Museum of Contemporary Art

I am at the exhibition of Mana Hatou, a Palestinian in exile. The pieces focue on being caged, in pain, struggling, and the difficulty of communication. There is a room filled with metal mesh boxes, like a battery hen farm, and one swinging lightbulb casting the barred shadows on the walls so you walk into a shifting cage.

A picture called 'Van Gogh's Back'; a man's hairy back made into swirls like the starry, starry night. A large circular container filled with sand has a rotating arm which carves furrows with one side and with the opposite side, smoothes the sand flat again.

I can see my life in this, a repetition of the same mistakes, a symbol of change and then wiped clear again. There was also a mirror with 'you are still here' written on it. I stood in front of it and was thankful.

*Joanna Penn, Diaries*

**Find ways to surprise yourself** with new and interesting knowledge or gorgeous pictures that lift you out of your present state. If you have an iPad, try the Flipboard app and check out some of the photography feeds or look online at Flickr.com for interesting new shots.

In the more physical world, old magazines are excellent for inspiration and can be bought very cheaply at charity shops. The pictures and articles are a rich source of information about the world and you can find things you didn't know about that may stimulate you in your own creativity. Patterns, colors, pictures of other places can be your inspiration for new goals and plans.

I love pictures of colorful clothes that would not fit in our Western offices – the indigo blue of the Moroccan Tuareg, the bright oranges of Hindu India, a clash of colors and patterns not favored in Western fashion but which can be inspirational for other designs.

(W) **What has inspired you to be creative in the past? Where can you find ideas for inspiration now? Make a date to go to an art gallery or research somewhere you can find inspiration.**

## Express yourself

Everyone is different and so we will all find our own way of investigating and expressing creativity. Here are some areas for exploration:

- Photography
- Collage
- Knitting/sewing
- Cooking
- Music
- Writing, poetry
- Making clothes

- Pottery *Sculpture
- Martial arts
- Dance
- Acting
- Singing
- Body painting
- {*insert your own idea here*}

Go to any community college, and look at the evening classes to find something that interests you. Check out your local papers for local classes/clubs. Everyone has an idea of something they want to try, so rediscover that deep down desire, or revisit that childhood fascination.

**If you don't think you have any talent, or that you can't do it well, it doesn't matter!**

Try anyway.

It is the attempt that frees fear and you may be surprised at what you discover. A friend of mine went along to a pottery class because she needed something creative in her life. She found a real love for it, eventually joining a more advanced class and now runs the local group. I have one of her pieces on my bookshelf and it's a fantastic reminder of a new start.

**Take pleasure in creativity for its own sake, and as a balance for your uninspiring day job.** No one need ever see your glorious colorful paintings, or your sketches, or your poetry. Be spontaneous and put color on the canvas or words on the page. See what it looks like, or what it says. If you let your mind run free, you may be surprised, at what appears. Be adventurous with your creativity. This is not a high risk or high expense activity. It is cheap therapy!

**You also never know where it might end up.**

In November 2009, I joined National Novel Writing Month (NaNoWriMo.org) to experiment with writing fiction. The aim was to write 50,000 words in the month of first draft material and see what happened. I managed 20,000 words and sparked the idea for my first novel, *Pentecost*. A year later, it was published on Amazon and has currently sold more than 35,000 copies. It became the basis of my ARKANE series of action-adventure thrillers and sparked a desire to write fiction as part of my creative career.

"Develop interest in life as you see it; in people, things, literature, music – the world is so rich, simply throbbing with rich treasures, beautiful souls and interesting people. Forget yourself."

*Henry Miller, Author*

**Creativity is also meant to be fun.**

I am definitely guilty of taking life too seriously and thinking that everything has to have a reason for doing it. I absolutely believe in creating things for sharing with others, but there's also the joy of creativity in and of itself. No pressure, just joy, and perhaps a little pride at what you have accomplished.

> **What do you do now that is creative? What did you love doing when you were a child? What would you like to do in the future for creative expression?**

## So, how do you apply creativity at work?

Any experience of creativity outside of work will affect your working life, even if it is just making you happier and more fulfilled because you are expanding yourself in a different way. Talking enthusiastically about your new passion for a creative project can lift your own day and make other people smile. They will look at you in surprise and recognize happiness.

Some companies work at fostering creativity in the workplace in order to create new products and gain a competitive advantage.

Google have a fantastic work practice of 20% time, where employees are allowed to work one day a week on projects they are passionate about, but that don't necessarily get developed into anything commercial. This empowers employees to express themselves, spend time away from their core projects and come up with creative and breakthrough ideas. This approach has led Google to such innovations as the searchable News site and Google Alerts.

Creativity is found in working environments where it is stimulated and encouraged. Rigid working situations are not conducive to creativity and it is realistic to say that many organizations do not even want creativity from their employees. Most are just focused on getting the job done within a tight time frame. If your company is one of these, then accept this and nurture your creative self outside of work.

Time also flies past and what do you have to show for your time at work?

Often, very little but the satisfaction of earning your living. On the other hand, **creative projects and the feelings they create endure.**

The exhaustion of repetitive work can kill creativity and passion if you don't spend time developing and nurturing your spark. **So incorporate some creativity into your daily life, and it will become something that recharges your batteries for life.**

 **How are you going to incorporate creativity into your life?**

"Art is the set of wings to carry you out of your own entanglement."

*Joseph Campbell*

# CHAPTER 9. ESCAPE IS SOMETIMES NECESSARY

"Life is either a daring adventure
or nothing at all."

*Helen Keller*

Enjoying your job is also about extending yourself outside work to add new facets to yourself and your life, so that work is not all you have. It's so easy to do everything without drawing breath and expend continuous effort, stopping only with exhaustion.

This kind of working life is not considered unusual today. People build up unspent leave time while they work crazy hours to keep to tight deadlines. Even if you go on leave, a week can fly by being tired or sick and then you have to go back to work.

When do we ever really stop?

(W) **When do we ever really stop?**

When do you actually have time to really relax and spend time considering your life?

Do you allow time for those internal changes that help to make sense of life?

Do you have real time for your family, or time for thinking about important things?

### If not now, then when?

It is important to take stock sometimes, and work out what is really important, to get some temporary escape from the hectic pace of our work. Here are some ideas to help you escape from the daily grind, starting close to home and then getting more adventurous.

## Escaping within the city

It is possible to find escape on your commute or near your home. Get lost looking out of the window instead of in a book or on the iPod. If you are in an urban concrete landscape, find a space where you can see the sky.

One day while writing this book, I made a list of all the things I could see on one morning commute that took me temporarily out of my miserable work situation. I saw:

- Bright flowers in window boxes along the railway line

- A magnolia tree hanging over the railing, petals falling onto the tracks

- The many different faces on the train, trying to guess their nationalities and what they did for work

- Graffiti art along the embankments. Lots of trash but some that made me think and question

- Crumbling houses covered in creepers, sparking images of hidden lives

- Restaurant signs in different languages, snapshots of other cultures

- A busker singing in the subway

- A Salvation Army man collecting donations with a wide smile on his face

- Striking modern offices making interesting silhouettes against the sky

- The sweet, condensed milk smell from a factory

Collecting lists like the one above places a focus on beauty and makes daily life more than just a grind. These specifics could be turned into a poem, story or painting. There is creative inspiration everywhere.

 **What can you see on your commute that is different or unusual?**

## Exploring the urban landscape

**Look around the streets or your workplace.** Cities often have their own form of beauty in modern architecture. The Chicago skyline for example, demonstrates that concrete, glass and steel can become something beautiful. Take note of what is around you.

Large cities all over the world are full of people from different places. **Learning about other cultures is a rich source of creativity, inspiration and escape.**

In the computer industry I worked with many Indian colleagues. I love the colorful Hindu festival of Diwali and also the amazing food. Different cultures have celebrations at different times of the year, so try asking people what they are celebrating. Most people are happy to explain what is going on. It's all about expanding your horizons closer to home.

There may be an area of your city that is home to other nationalities where you can go to be immersed in a different culture. Within the shops and restaurants of another culture, you can find little parts of other countries. For a brief time, you can experience a taste of that far-off place. For example, in Auckland,

New Zealand you can visit the Pacific Island markets with Fijian, Tongan and Samoan people and then go to the French market in a different part of town for croissants and café-au-lait.

> (w) **Which areas of your city/town are home to different cultures? Make a date to go and walk there/go for a meal.**

You may have to search, but you can find a retreat even in the most congested of cities. Many cities have parks and even city farms you can escape to when things get too much and you want to relax somewhere green. Maybe it's a local park, a shady walk or somewhere you have to drive to, or catch the train/bus for the day.

## "See the world in a grain of sand and heaven in a wild flower, hold infinity in the palm of your hand, and eternity in an hour."
### *William Blake*

There are botanic gardens in urban spaces with foreign hothouse flowers to brighten your day. In England, there are arboretums – whole forests of different types of trees where you can walk. Walking among huge, leafy trees can ground you, making you feel rooted in the earth you walk on and giving you some much needed perspective.

Everyone needs a little nature, especially in our highly technological world. You will crave it even if you don't realize it, and without it, you will lack a sense of peace. Walking in nature is a healing, meditative process where things can be worked out in your mind without you even realizing it.

## Weybridge, England

My walk to work from the train station is crunchy frosty, my breath freezing on the air and I keep my hands deep in my pockets in the warm. I have a horse-chestnut in my pocket that I found one day – it's smooth, cool, fits in my palm so nicely, a comforting solidarity. I has gone from the dark brown of the nut from the shell to a lighter colour, the whorls and patters of the grain are the insides of a mini tree. It gives me a sense of nature in my cornered life. I keep it until the glossy sheen begins to fade and then I find a new one, fresh out of the shell, to hold like a talisman against the grey.

*Joanna Penn, Diaries*

If you can't make it out into nature, how about watching it on TV or DVD?

The BBC's 'Blue Planet' is one of my favorite series as it looks at the oceans, the species within them, the depths and the shores. Nature gives you perspective on life by taking you out of your situation and into wonder, awe and respect. How many other species are living their own lives without any knowledge of yours?

**Feeling insignificant on the face of the planet can sometimes bring perspective to the situations you find yourself in.**

(w) **Where can you go locally that will help you escape into nature? Book a time in your diary and commit to taking time out.**

## Micro Adventures

Adventurer Alastair Humphreys has cycled around the world, walked across India and rowed the Atlantic, but he also advocates micro-adventures. These are little experiences which are close to home but still push the boundaries of the comfort zone. They can be free or cheap, shorter or longer, but they don't take a plane flight or vacation time to experience.

Some of the micro-adventures Alastair has undertaken have included:

- Entering a race locally

- Eating in restaurants from global cultures starting with A to Z

- Walking around the boundary of the M25 (motorway around London) in midwinter

- Exploring an island

- Wild swimming in rivers

- Grabbing a map. Closing your eyes. Pointing and going.

> **"You do not need to fly to the other side of the planet to do an expeditin. You do not need to be an elite athlete, expertly trained, or rich to have an adventure. Adventure is only a state of mind.**
>
> *Alastair Humphreys,*
> *Adventurer, Author, Speaker*

## Getting away from it all

Sometimes, if you cannot find joy in your job, you may need to just get away from it all. Work can be made bearable if you set deadlines for yourself to take a break at regular intervals. You then have something to work towards. Travel is a continuum where there are options for all situations and budgets.

- Long weekend / mini-break. Weekends are so often taken up by the chores and responsibilities you have to do just to keep life running, so that you don't get a real chance to relax. A long weekend or mini-break of 3-4 days can give you the opportunity to get away. It is long enough to fly somewhere or take a longer drive, stay overnight in a different situation and take time to relax, or be with family and friends.

- Two weeks holiday. One week off work is not long enough to do much except catch up on sleep, paperwork and all the home-based jobs you've put off for so long. Often people become ill on a one week holiday once the body realizes its time to stop. It is just long enough to start relaxing and then you are back at work. So, make sure you always take two weeks if you actually want a proper break, then you can make it into relaxation by the second week and spend some time thinking.

- Going traveling. This book is primarily about change, and sometimes there is no other way to make big changes in your life than to get out of where you are right now.

- Leaving a job is a big decision, but leaving your life behind for a time is a greater challenge and often gives you more time to think away from the situation.

**I use to work in London, England at a high stress, long hours job and one day I realised that I just worked, drank too much, recovered and repeated the cycle. I was doing too much at work, and nothing outside of work except drinking and watching TV.**

**I burnt myself out after two and a half years of this life. I resigned and went to Western Austrailia to leran to scuba dive and to be in the bush for a few months. I needed space and silence, to get away from work, alcohol and escapist behaviour. I wanted to see beauty and get away from concrete, to stop conforming to what we are all 'meant to do'. I needed to get away to find some clarity.**

*Joanna Penn, Diaries*

**It seems easier to make big life decisions when you are traveling.**

There is time to think on buses, trains and planes, when you are waiting for the next move, and you can talk to people who are living different lives. There is the freedom to tell anyone anything as you know you are unlikely to ever see them again. Being able to say "I'm doing nothing right now" is fine on the road. People are more likely to ask where you are going than what job you do.

**The act of physically moving on can sometimes help release what is blocking us inside** and we find ourselves someone different on our return. The change in the external environment enables internal change.

I am not suggesting that everyone resign from their jobs and go traveling, just that sometimes you need a decent break away in order to think about the big picture and what you want next.

If you have a partner, children, a mortgage, and other responsibilities, it's about deciding what is best for everyone. There has to be time to discuss these important things together. Some people aim to do this at retirement. When people have finished their commitments to work and family, they can then downsize, or move to the coast, or travel to countries they have dreamed of.

**But what do they miss out on if they wait until then?**

**Are there places that you have always wanted to go?**

**Travel allows you to literally leave your baggage behind.** Travelers take the bare minimum and acquire anything else on the journey. You often don't need as much as you think.

Travel enables you to live in the moment. You may have plans for where you are going, but there is no stress because it doesn't matter if you don't get there.

**There is a form of healing in travel,** taking you from your comfort zone into a place where you have to live on the edge. Stereotypes are questioned. You are the foreigner, and simple things become more complex. When you don't know the language and you need a bed for the night, you can find out the life skills you really have, or need to learn. You reach out to other people for help, and generally people are amazing in responding to you.

**It is in being closer to the edge that you learn more about yourself.**

**Travel is self-development without a real curriculum.** You will be grateful for the unexpected happenings and the experience of things you didn't plan for. These experiences will stretch, challenge and change you.

At some point, you will have to return to the life of responsibility and work. You will need to get back to family and friends, the money will run out, or you will have your answers. It may be that you just want to go home. On returning from a travel experience, you can often see life with more clarity and are able to put things into perspective.

I left London for Australia in 2000, resigning from a consulting job on my 25th birthday to go and find change and adventure. What started as travel morphed into another life down under, with seven years in New Zealand and four in Australia. I returned to London in 2011, a different person with a new perspective and a new, creative career.

**Travel changes you. I really believe that, and sometimes it's all we need to reset our lives and find happiness again.**

 **Is there an opportunity for travel in your life? Can you make one?**

"Change is the only thing worth living for. Never sit your life out at a desk. Ulcers and heart condition follow.

*Bruce Chatwin*

# Part 3:
# How to change your career... and your life

# CHAPTER 10. WHAT DO YOU REALLY WANT TO DO?

People who love their jobs often talk about the opportunities and challenges that come their way, the interests they have that their job relates to and how suited they are to the work they do. But you may not feel you are at this point yet.

Part of enjoying your job now is about knowing that you have somewhere to move on to, that you have a plan for the future and that you are not stuck in this particular job forever. This section is for those people who feel they want a new role or a new job entirely, perhaps even in a different industry.

## "Your electricity might flow better through another socket."
### *Donald Trump*

In asking people what they really want to do, there are usually only two answers.

a)  I know what I want to do; I just don't know how to get there.

b)  I don't know what I want to do – but I do know it is not what I am doing right now!

Both groups of people continue at the job they have fallen into because they think someday they will make a change, but not right now because there are bills to pay. Yet they may not know what they want to do until they try some new things and see what happens.

**If you don't know what you want to do, it is important to spend some time getting to know yourself,** really thinking about <u>you</u> and what you are like. Not what you think you <u>should</u> be, but about who you really are and who you want to be. You need to think about what you want in your job, and where you want to take your life. Then you need to start off in one direction and adjust your path along the way.

It's a bit like skiing. You have to have momentum in order to turn, so you need to get moving, even if your initial direction doesn't take you directly downhill.

Think about these four broad directions.

**WHAT DO YOU WANT?**

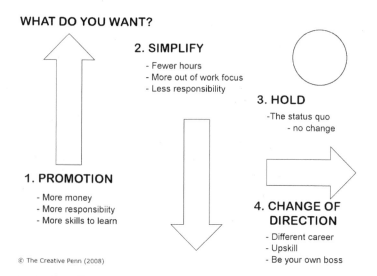

**2. SIMPLIFY**
- Fewer hours
- More out of work focus
- Less responsibility

**3. HOLD**
-The status quo
- no change

**1. PROMOTION**
- More money
- More responsibiity
- More skills to learn

**4. CHANGE OF DIRECTION**
- Different career
- Upskill
- Be your own boss

© The Creative Penn (2008)

ⓦ **As you read these sections, decide which category you fit into.**

## 1. Promotion

Do you want to earn more money, have more responsibility, or higher status in your organization or field?

Are you willing to up-skill, put in the hours and learn new things in order to be promoted?

This may be a promotion in your current job, or with another company. The key is that you want to be moving up in your chosen area. If you are happy with what you are doing as a job, then focus on developing yourself further in order to take advantage of promotions (Chapter 3) as well as setting goals and focusing on achievement (Chapter 13).

ⓦ **If you are aiming for promotion, what specifically do you need to focus on to get there?**

## 2. Simplify

Do you want to have more of a relaxed life outside work or have less responsibility? Do you need less stress and more time? Are you willing to accept a change in your financial situation to achieve this?

There are various options for simplifying your work life.

- Four-day week/ part-time work. If you work fewer than five days a week, you will have that extra day to relax or do other activities. There are huge benefits to working part time, including the extra energy you have available for yourself, your family and your other personal commitments. Another form of part-time work is job sharing which is becoming especially popular when people have young families. Make sure you cut down the amount of work you are meant to achieve in the reduced days or you will still be stressed. This one thing changed my life substantially. Back in 2007, I moved to four days per week as an IT consultant in order to spend the other day focusing on writing, blogging and growing my online business. It gave me the energy I needed to break through the initial inertia and write my first book. You can read more about this in the bonus interview on career change.

- Work from home some days. Working from home reduces commuting time, which can give you more freedom and quality of life. Many workplaces are offering more flexible working conditions in order to improve retention, so it is worth asking for what you want. You may be surprised how easy this is to implement and what a difference it makes to your life. Make sure you have an area for work that is separate from your family life so you don't end up working longer hours instead.

- Take a less stressful job with less responsibility. Are you willing to trade a higher income or status for a more simple life that would allow more quality time? This option means a change in attitude and possibly lifestyle. You may need to be more structured with your finances in order to accomplish this, but it will be worthwhile if you consider your time most important.

(W)

**If you would like to simplify, what options could you consider to make this happen in your working life?**

## 3. Hold

This is maintaining the status quo, staying where you are and continuing on your current path at work. This may be the right option for you as you think about the changes you want to make.

But remember, this can only be temporary. The world doesn't stay still and change is inevitable. So, come back to this chapter in the future if your situation changes, because the status quo doesn't last long.

## 4. Change Direction

Do you want to do something completely different?

Maybe a different career, or starting your own business, or moving to another area or country?

**This option involves reinventing yourself** and breaking out of the stereotypes you may hold about work and what you can do. It will involve changing your mindset and perhaps re-training. A change in direction can also be combined with promotion or simplifying.

There may also be false starts on the journey as you discover more about yourself.

I found I wasn't happy in the corporate career within two years of leaving University, but it took me another ten years of experimentation before I finally found what I was looking for in being an author-entrepreneur. Over that interim period, I tried many different businesses. In the next chapter, I explore what it means to be an entrepreneur and there's a case-study of my current business, The Creative Penn Limited in the bonus chapters.

**We are complex people,** and making a living at what you love is definitely difficult. But you don't know unless you try! I understand the false starts and the difficulties but it is worth it to pursue the goal.

The following section will guide you through the areas you need to focus on in order to find out what you really want to do. At least it will start you on the journey.

**W** In going through this process, it is helpful to write down the answers so you can refer to them later. Your thoughts will change over time but it is useful to follow the process. I have added in some of my thoughts so you can see real examples.

## What do I want to do?

© The Creative Penn (2008)

## What did I want to be when I was a child/teenager?

When you were young, you didn't have to worry about the practicalities of living, working or earning money. When you thought about your future, it was not constrained by reality in any way. This is the time you dreamt and imagined. Everyone grows up and changes but there is still some of that imaginative child left in you who can help you to access what you want to do next.

 **Write down all the things you wanted to be or do when you were young.**

Think back: it doesn't matter how impractical the ideas are.

What do your early choices reveal about your personality and what you might want to do now?

I always wanted to be an author and later found a passion for psychology and then scuba diving. All of those things have found their way into my previous work choices and current life.

## What do I like doing now? What am I passionate about?

Consider what you really enjoy right now, or what you used to enjoy when you had more time. Make a list of anything that makes you smile and that you look forward to doing. What do you talk about in a passionate way? What makes your face light up when you discuss it?

Here are some examples:

- Fishing, hiking, swimming, surfing, diving

- Reading, writing, making clothes, gardening, doing puzzles

- Being with my partner, children and my family

- Making things, fixing things around the house

- Helping people

- Making money, investing, renovating houses

Obviously, there are so many more!

**List everything you love doing now. Don't censor yourself.**

## What parts of my job do I enjoy? What do I want in my perfect working situation?

Most people enjoy parts of their job, or can at least see the benefits. These are the things you want to keep hold of and make sure you still have even if you change direction. They can be a starting point for helping you find what you really want in a perfect job.

Write down the aspects of the job you enjoy. Examples may include:

- Working with people or in a team

- Health plan or benefits

- short commute

- Working outdoors

- Helping people

Don't let these examples constrain you. Just write down whatever comes to mind, however small.

**What parts of your job do you enjoy? What do you want in your perfect working situation?**

I have been refining my list for years now. I want to be living a creative life, writing and publishing books and courses. I also like public speaking, so my perfect working situation includes this too. I want to be flexible with my time, working hard for some periods and then taking chunks of time out. I like to travel, but only for experiences or retreats to gorgeous places, not corporate hotels. I like being in the center of things, with access to cultural places and opportunities for events and networking.

## What do I hate/ definitely NOT want to do?

Think about what you react negatively to, for example:

- Don't like blood – so you don't want to be a doctor/dentist/surgeon/vet

- Not good with numbers – so not an accountant

- Hard, physical work – so you don't want to be a gardener

Write down the jobs that you would not want to do, or the types of activity you would hate. You need to decide what you won't compromise on, and what you definitely will not do, even for a lot of money.

 **What do you hate doing? What will you not compromise on?**

For me, freedom is one of my highest values ,so anything curtailing that is a no-no. Because of this I decided not to be tied to a physical location when designing my business. I don't like being an employee and I don't want to have employees, so I will always contract and hire contractors. I don't like pointless 'busy-work' where I'm not adding value, so I don't like office face-time. I want to be paid for my creative output and results, not on being somewhere for a specific number of hours. This manifests in my own business as not holding physical stock or shipping books/goods to people. I'm not interested in posting and packing so that must be outsourced or use online options.

## What do other people say I am good at?

It is very likely that people will have said to you at some point "You are so good at _____."

 **Write down what those things are.**

Are they actually things you like being good at? Why are you good at them? Is it because you have spent time gaining these skills? Or is it a personality trait, e.g. being good at listening?

Are these things you would like to incorporate into your future work?

## What specific skills do I have or what could I develop?

To identify your skills, think back over what you have done in your life. The following categories may help.

- Qualifications/certificates/diplomas/licenses

- Physical skills e.g. ability to drive, outdoor skills

- Personal skills e.g. ability to communicate, customer service, patience

- Job experience skills e.g. word processing skills

- Computer skills e.g. able to use Microsoft Word, ability to use the internet for research

- Other abilities that might be useful e.g. I speak Spanish, I can play the piano, I can build flat-pack furniture

Also, you might be willing to learn, so think about what else you might enjoy.

I didn't know anything about internet marketing four years ago. Now I am an international speaker who keynotes on this topic. I also didn't know how to create and edit video but now I produce multimedia courses. I didn't have those skills but I learned them because they fitted with the type of business I wanted to have.

> **(W)** **List everything, even if you don't think it is that important.**

You don't know yet where these answers might lead to. Again, don't censor or underestimate yourself. Just get it all out on the page so you can review it later.

## Do I want to be employed by someone else or be my own boss?

This is a key question and should be asked even if you have never considered working for yourself.

**Studies show that many self-employed people enjoy their jobs more, because they have greater control over their work and know that their individual effort actually affects their bottom line.** They have greater freedom to work when they want, but many work far longer hours than employees in order to keep the business going.

In comparison, many employees like the security and ease of having a company pay their salary and manage their taxes. They also enjoy the knowledge of where they will be working, how many hours and what the career path might look like.

I go into the Entrepreneurial option in detail in Chapter 11 as it is where I feel most fulfilled. But I also know people who prefer to be an employee. Being in someone else's company means you can focus on working in the business, not on the business. You can be a specialist without having to worry about all the peripheries of sales, marketing, finance and production, or where the next dollar is coming from. There are pros and cons on both sides, and so both should be considered.

Do you like being an employee? Do you want to work for yourself? What are the pros and cons of both of these options for you personally?

 **List everything, even if you don't think it is that important.**

## What are my priorities and practicalities?

It is important to look at your priorities in life as well as the practicalities that set boundaries around what you will aim for.

**This is not to say you shouldn't aim for the stars, but there must be some reality in what you aim to achieve.**

For example, if you have young children, your priority may be to stay at home with them in the short term. This doesn't stop you starting the process of changing your job, but it is unlikely that you can drop everything and take a job in another country, or even work at the weekends, as this is not practical.

**What are your priorities? What practicalities and constraints do you need to consider?**

 **What are your priorities? What practicalities and constraints do you need to consider?**

## What do I want to achieve, and by when?

It is important to think about your whole life in context. Often, people just get on with their day-to-day life and forget to look ahead to plan the future.

When you look back at age 65 or 70, will you have achieved what you set out to do? Or will you realize you have been working at something you didn't like for the last 45-50 years?

**What do you want to achieve for the rest of your life?**

Many people say they want to provide for their families, but at some point, your dependents will be independent. So if your main aim is to support a family, you also need to think about how you want to do that. Is it possible to achieve this AND do something you love?

(W) **What do you want to achieve? When do you want to achieve this by?**

## Now collate the results

By now you should have spent quality time thinking about these questions and have a lot of notes. These will give you an insight into your skills and preferences, as well as what you currently want and don't want in your work.

(W) **Read back over your answers and add anything else that comes to mind.**

**These results are important to hold onto, even if you don't use them right now.** Keep them somewhere safe and add to them when you can. If you open your mind to the opportunities around you, you will see possibilities you had never thought of before, and find answers to add to your questions.

"Success is liking yourself, liking what you do, and liking how you do it."

*Maya Angelou*

# CHAPTER 11. ENTREPRENEURSHIP OR WORKING FOR YOURSELF

There is no longer a 'job for life' as there might have been in the past, and there is likely to be little or no State pension at the end of our working lives. Loyalty is not rewarded anymore, either within companies towards individuals or vice versa. We are now completely responsible for our own careers and for making the changes necessary in order to sustain our incomes and lifestyle.

There is no stability in full-time employment. Having a contract or long-term tenure doesn't make you immune to changes in the market which may lead to widespread redundancy and outsourcing.

Finally, there is a widespread malaise in the corporate world, where people are wondering whether what they are doing is worthwhile. Many are searching for something more meaningful to do with their lives.

This is a time of incredible flux in the world as globalization and technology change the way people work. Traditional education is failing people, but there are myriad opportunities emerging in areas unheard of ten years ago.

Change isn't something to be scared of.

These days people are likely to have several careers in their lifetimes, and many will try working for themselves. It's an opportunity for you to develop into a more self-reliant and independent person and perhaps to find that you prefer being your own boss.

You may stay in full-time employment and develop an alternative business on the side. This way you can grow multiple income streams which will also offset the risk of losing full-time employment. You may also stumble upon something you really love to do in the process.

In this chapter, I explore some of the positives and negatives of being an entrepreneur working for yourself. I also give some details of how I run my business as an example. Maybe this will help you decide whether this is a path you want to experiment with for yourself.

## What is an entrepreneur anyway?

You might consider the word 'entrepreneur' too much for a little idea you have about working from home, but the definition is basically someone who turns ideas into income. That could be you.

There are many options for running your own business. What you decide on depends on these key factors:

(1) What are you good at?

(2) What do you love to do?

(3) What does the market want or need?

(4) Education in the skills you need to run a business, including the financials.

**It's important to consider all the angles because you don't want to just end up creating another day job.** One of the benefits of working for yourself is the enjoyment that comes from doing something you love or that is fulfilling for you.

But many of the problems small businesses face is that people forget question (3) what does the market want and often skip education in business skills (4). I definitely fell into this trap and so I share my early business failures later in this chapter.

## What are the types of business that entrepreneurs create?

### (a) Expert becomes sole trader or small company - doing the same job

One of the most common startup businesses is when an expert working for a company moves to being self-employed doing essentially the same job.

For example, you work as a financial advisor in a company but want to go freelance; or you're a plumber working for a company who now wants to run your own business. Maybe you have worked in an office and now become a virtual assistant, doing similar work but for people all over the world from the comfort of your home.

For example, I was a contract IT consultant for 5 years. I had my own company but all it did was employ me and bill my services. I outsourced the accounting and company side of things. I had no employees. This set up made me happier than being an employee, as I was paid for the hours I worked, so I had a lot more control.

Some people take this further and create a bigger business. For example, an accountant starts to freelance and then develops a small business accounting firm.

The best book to read about the potential problems with this business model is *The E-Myth* by Michael Gerber. Basically, he says that you can be an expert at something without being able to run a business doing the same thing. You might be a great baker, but not be able to run a bakery. You might be a great computer programmer, but that doesn't mean you can run a company of computer programmers.

**The skills you need to run a company successfully are not the same as those needed to run a company successfully.** If you are thinking of creating a business from your existing expertise, then make sure you get the education you need to run your business, or outsource it to a company that can do it for you.

## (b) Start-ups and small companies: product or service centric

Some people have fantastic ideas for start-ups, selling new products or services that they are inspired to take to market. This can be as simple as creating a product at the kitchen table to solve a problem that others are suffering too. Think Sara Blakely, who started Spanx slimming undergarments by cutting the feet off a pair of pantyhose and is now the youngest billionaire ever.

A business can start small but can grow into something bigger, at which point it may need investment funding and a team of people to put the project together. There are high risks but also high rewards to this larger type of business.

## (c) Online businesses

Since the explosion of the internet, social networking, smart phones, and tablets, there have been an increasing number of online businesses and start-ups that don't rely on physical products to produce income.

The ease of creation online as well as the low cost of entry means that ideas are only limited by the imagination. People create games and apps, business software or online services. There are no barriers either, in terms of age or experience, in a world of high tech and can-do thinking. Think Mark Zuckerberg with Facebook, or the smaller success of the designers of the Angry Birds game, now a global product brand.

This book can only be a catalyst to help you take the next step in the journey. There are many other books you can read on how to start a business. Check the Resources section for more information.

## What are the pros and cons of being an entrepreneur or working for yourself?

There are always positives and negatives in any job or life choice, so it's important to consider both sides.

**Pros**

- You're **independent** and can spend your time on your passion.

- You have the **freedom** to do what you want, when you want and be based where you want.

- Your working hours can be **flexible** and fit in with the other priorities in your life. You are in control of your stress levels.

- You can do **meaningful work**, instead of the pointless busy-work that so often defines many jobs. You don't have to sit in boring meetings, or write long documents that nobody reads or cares about.

- You don't report to anyone else but yourself and can **choose** the people you work with. You don't have to put up with workplace bullies, laziness or bad management.

- You can **make decisions fast** and move quickly into new opportunities without asking permission.

- Your **income potential is not limited** by the constraints of a salary band.

- You are **empowered** and **in control** of your own future, not subject to the whims of a company.

- You can be endlessly **creative**.

## Cons

- You are responsible for your earnings. If you're not earning, it's your responsibility. **No one pays you** for a holiday or a sick day.

- There is **no security or stability** in your income. It's actually much easier to have a traditional job, or a string of them as you know when the money is coming in and can plan accordingly. You also have **no benefits** package, so you need to budget for healthcare and saving for your retirement.

- You are running a business, so **you have to learn about all aspects, including finance, sales and marketing.** You also have to pay your own taxes, and ensure all the 'back end' **administration and record-keeping** is completed correctly. This has been the downfall of many an entrepreneur who has not kept an eye on the accounts. You can hire professionals for this or work with a partner who has a different skill-set, but it has to get done somehow.

- **It's hard to get started.** Many entrepreneurs end up working far longer hours than people in traditional jobs, especially at the beginning.

(W) | **What are the pros and cons in your situation, both for staying in your job and working for yourself?**

## The Entrepreneurial Mindset

Being an entrepreneur is not for everyone. There are a lot of responsibilities but personally, I know it is where I belong. I would go as far as to say I am practically unemployable as an employee these days. I just don't fit into any corporate organizational model anymore (nor do I want to!). Here are some of the aspects of the entrepreneurial mindset. These may already be part of you or develop over time as you experiment with opportunity.

### Desire to be independent and create something new.

There has to be something that sparks the entrepreneurial spirit, the desire to start something yourself. Perhaps this is part of every person, but society beats it out of us over time. Before large global companies, everyone worked for themselves or in small cooperatives, so entrepreneurship is our natural state. Once you recognize this need within yourself, you can begin to act on it.

### Drive to achieve.

You need to have a can-do attitude and a drive to succeed and achieve. There will be many obstacles along the way and you need the perseverance to get yourself through. If you don't have this type of drive, entrepreneurship may not be for you, or it may be that you haven't found the right opportunity yet.

### Passion vs. Work/Life Balance.

When you have a day job, everyone talks about work/life balance, mainly because most people don't like their jobs and they desperately need something else to make it all worthwhile. When you have a passion that becomes your work, you don't feel this need. In fact, your passion drives you to spend a lot of time on your business, especially at the beginning as you build it up. Personally,

I believe this is part of why you start your own business. You are so passionate, you don't want to do anything else. Obviously you need some balance in terms of time with your family and friends, as well as sleep, but any 'spare' time inevitably is spent on the idea or business because that's what you are passionate about.

## Know yourself and work with a team.

There are things you are good at, and some things you need to hire people for. It's important to know when you need to pay someone else. For example, do you want to learn the technical aspects of building a website or do you want to pay someone for that? Do you want to become a tax expert, or do you want to pay an accountant? I am a writer and so I hire professional editors and book cover designers to help make my books into a quality product. I also pay for transcription services and I have a virtual assistant who helps with running my site. Spend some time getting to know yourself and what you can do yourself or what you need others for.

## Be constantly learning.

Successful entrepreneurs are always learning and love to find out new things. Having a beginner's mind is an asset. It doesn't matter if you don't know something as there's always a way to find out. Always be asking questions and seeking out why things work or don't work. You can always apply successful principles from other businesses to your own. Model the success of other entrepreneurs, even outside your niche.

## Understand it's about sales and marketing, as well as 'doing.'

Businesses need cashflow, so they need customers or some kind of funding. Sales and marketing are fundamental aspects of business, and many people resist learning these skills, associating them with car salesmen or sleazy advertising. But these days, marketing is more about relationships, social networking and content marketing - the provision of useful information or entertainment to attract attention. Whatever your business, sales and marketing is a critical aspect.

## Understanding the Compound Effect.

Overnight success often comes after years of hard work, putting in long hours, with risks taken and difficulties overcome. Sometimes it seems that you are not moving forward fast enough for what you want to achieve. In the fantastic book, The Compound Effect, author Darren Hardy talks about the tiny increments of change over time that result in long-term success. It's not exciting or sexy but it's a combination of choices, habits and momentum that compound over time into something significant.

One example is becoming a professional writer. It comes from writing words every day, even just 1000 a day, that combine over time into a finished book, and then another one, and then another one, while the writer improves every day. Tiny steps, but incrementally, they build an exciting future.

 **Do you have an entrepreneurial mindset? Or how can you develop one?**

## Many businesses fail

Studies have shown that three out of every five new businesses fail. But that statistic doesn't account for the fact that most entrepreneurs start something else. The Creative Penn is my fifth business, so you could say the first four were 'failures.' But it's important to remember that failure isn't a bad thing. It's how we learn and grow. It's also better to fail fast, so you can learn your lessons and move on. Sometimes we don't know ourselves well enough to understand what we really want (check out Chapter 10 if this is you!)

> ### "I have not failed. I've just found 10,000 ways that won't work."
>
> #### *Thomas Edison*

Here are my four previous business attempts and the lessons I learned from them. I hope this helps you avoid some of my mistakes.

Keep in mind the four critical factors as you read through:

(1) What are you good at?

(2) What do you love?

(3) What does the market want/need?

(4) Education in the skills you need to run a business, including the financials.

## Boutique travel itineraries for New Zealand

When I moved to New Zealand in 2001, I was creating a lot of travel itineraries for friends so I decided to put them on a website and try to sell them. That was before website creation and maintenance became as easy as it is today, so I hired someone to design it for me. I was working full-time so it was all done on the side. It only lasted three months, as I just wasn't that interested. When I had my first customer, I discovered the tiny margins I would make. That type of material was increasingly available for free and travel agents were already doing what I was trying to do. It had a reasonably low start-up cost but didn't go anywhere.

This mainly failed on (2) as well as (4) since I didn't do the figures on the business.

## Luxury charter and scuba diving business

My husband at the time was a Dive Instructor and experienced charter boat skipper and I am a PADI Divemaster. We loved the New Zealand Bay of Islands and we had access to a luxury launch we could rent for the days we could charter it, so we started a luxury scuba diving company. We had big dreams of spending our days on the ocean, earning a great living with a fantastic lifestyle. It was an idyllic dream but the reality was brutal.

There were many problems with the business model.

First, it had high fixed and variable costs, including insurance and fuel bills that kept rising. We also needed expensive dive gear, as customers expected that to be provided. Getting charters through travel companies meant they took a high commission so our pricing was difficult. We also had to advertise to get bookings. The New Zealand weather is also highly variable so some trips didn't live up to customer expectations, and our love of diving became a chore.

The business was also crucially dependent on another person, who eventually lost interest. We spent a lot of money, time and effort on the business. I funded it through working full-time as an IT consultant, with weekends on the boat. It was exhausting and 'failed' within six months. The dream just didn't match the reality.

Yet I am so grateful for this experience. I learned that I don't want such a high-risk business. I don't want to be tied to a physical location with expensive assets, running costs and maintenance. I don't want to be dependent on someone else who could destroy what we had built. These are critically important aspects of business that you should also make decisions about if you go down the entrepreneurial route.

This business failed on (1) and (4) but mainly on (4). If we had done a serious business plan and really understood the financials, we never would have proceeded.

## Property investor

You might remember the books and the hype around property back in the early 2000s. It seemed as if property prices would just keep on rising, and with a little effort, you could renovate properties and sell them on or make income from rental that could generate significant wealth. The global financial crisis of 2008 and the sub-prime mortgage debacle put a real brake on property investment. Of course, some people did well and there is still money to be made, but for small-time investors, it has been a difficult time.

With my husband's renovation skills, we tried the property game on two occasions, but both times it didn't pay off because of a myriad of reasons. It's a long-term strategy for capital gain but we ended up funding the shortfall in mortgage cost, so it was never a viable business because of negative cashflow.

This failed on (1) because we just weren't 'good' at property and that we couldn't sustain it for the long term. We did spend a lot of time and money learning about it (4) but there is a great deal of ongoing due diligence and patience involved in expert property investment. It also failed on (2), as it was always a wealth creation strategy and not something we loved, so the passion was never there to constantly be on the lookout for opportunity.

## Contract IT consultant

This was the classic model of an expert practitioner working for a company becoming an expert practitioner working for herself. All I did was continue my IT work but under my own company name, mainly so I could have more freedom. I didn't want to work five days a week or continue with the bureaucratic side of being an employee. I didn't want a career path in corporate organizations, so I treated it as a day job, something short term while I worked on other things on the side. I did an excellent job but I didn't invest my own time in further education or career advancement in this area. For those of you who might work in IT, I was an SAP Financials consultant specializing in banking systems and Accounts Payable. Sounds exciting, right!

This book was originally written because of how unhappy I was as an IT consultant, but this work did pay the bills for thirteen years. It funded my other experiments including the development of my current business. I left because of (2): I never loved it. I enjoyed a lot of it, especially the people, but I never felt passionate about what I did. Perhaps this can't be described as a failure, more as something I tried many times to leave and finally made it out of in 2011.

So that's my journey of 'failure', which I share because many entrepreneurs have such a journey. Some failure is spectacular, costing people their fortunes. Mine have been modest setbacks in that context, but still there have been difficult times where I have gone back to IT yet again in order to start anew.

I'm sure I still have failures ahead of me, but for my current business model, read the next chapter which is an in-depth case study of The Creative Penn Limited.

W

**What lessons have you learned from 'failures' in your past? How could you use that information to steer your path for the future?**

## Don't give up the day job

I don't like risk, which is why I always kept my day job while experimenting with business ideas. I only gave up IT consulting after The Creative Penn had been running for three years and was bringing in an income. I also saved a buffer of cash in order to cushion the change.

If you want to start your own business and you can't tolerate much risk, I recommend doing it this way, as it removes the horrific pressure of having to pay the bills. Desperation is not fun, especially if you have a family to feed and a mortgage to pay. I changed to working four days a week in order to give myself more time to create, and I go into this more in the bonus interviews included at the end of the book.

## Questions to ask yourself if you are considering entrepreneurship

The following questions are in the Companion Workbook so you can download to write in if you prefer.

### Overarching Questions:

- What are my personal lifestyle goals and how does the business idea fit into this?

- Where do I want to be in five years? Who do I want to be?

- What do I like doing?

- What am I good at?

- What does the market need or want? Is there a niche that already exists but hasn't caught fire yet?

- Do I have the skills and education needed to start this business? How can I educate myself further? Do I know what I need to know about starting a business?

- What am I willing to give up for this to succeed?

- What is my tolerance for risk?

- What does success look like for me? *(This is important as you will need a very different business model if being a multi-millionaire with a flash car is your goal vs someone who wants to live simply and spend 3 months a year traveling.)*

- What word encapsulates my highest value?
  *(After a lot of soul searching, I decided that my word is freedom – of time and physical place. This has guided my whole business model so it is worth thinking about.)*

- Do I have the support of my family/friends or a social network of likeminded people to keep me motivated?

## Financial Questions:

- Can I lower my living costs so I have less financial pressure?

- How much money do I <u>need</u> every month? i.e. I must make this to live.

- How much money do I <u>want</u> every month? i.e. What I would like to make in order to have some fun and a better lifestyle. *This should be a realistic goal, not the dream of multi-millions at this stage!*

- What are the overheads of this business? What are the fixed and variable costs?

- What do I have in place as a safety net to make the transition if I am going to give up my job?

- How do I actually get paid? Do I need to set up specific banking arrangements or a PayPal account or shopping cart?

- Do I need a loan? If so, how does that work in my financial plan for the next few years?

## Business Questions:

- Who are my customers? Who will pay me for this product/service?

- What are the aims of my business? What do I want to achieve?

- Do I operate as a sole trader or shall I start a company? *(You will most likely need professional business and tax advice to make this decision as there are all kinds of ramifications.)*

- Can I do this while I work full-time or could I move to part-time work for a while?

- Where do I want to be located, or do I want to be location independent?

- If I have a physical product, how does the manufacturing and shipping work? Do I need to hold physical stock or can I use outsourcing and drop-shipping?

- Do I want or need employees? Could I use contract services or virtual workers?

- How will people find my business? *(This is all about marketing and how you will get your product/service in front of potential customers.)*

These questions are by no means exhaustive, but they give you a good indication of the things you need to consider. If you're interested in how I run my business now, you can check out a case study of my current business, The Creative Penn Limited in the **Bonus chapters at the back.**

> **"Ideas can be life-changing. Sometimes all you need to open the door is just one more good idea."**
>
> *Jim Rohn*

# CHAPTER 12. THE CAREER CHANGE PROCESS

Now you have decided what you want to do, this chapter focuses on the actions you need to take to implement the change process in your working life. The flow diagram below represents the steps you need to take in order to turn the ideas you have into reality. Don't worry if you are not 100% sure yet: all you need is an initial direction in which to head.

**Great things happen in your life when you make them happen!**

Take the first step and you will find the next steps will be revealed to you.

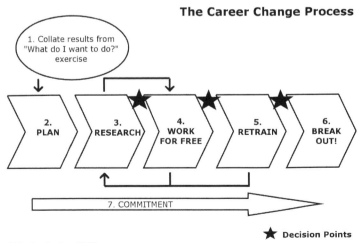

**The Career Change Process**

1. Collate results from "What do I want to do?" exercise

2. PLAN

3. RESEARCH

4. WORK FOR FREE

5. RETRAIN

6. BREAK OUT!

7. COMMITMENT

★ Decision Points

© The Creative Penn (2008)

**(W)** This process and associated questions and exercises are all contained within the Companion Workbook available on the website www.TheCreativePenn.com/careerchange

# (1) Look at your results from the previous chapter "What do I want to do for my job?"

Look at everything you have written about yourself and distill those answers into a few key points about yourself and potential jobs. Make it short and concise, for example:

I'm good with my hands

I like working with people and helping them

My priority is to make money and provide for my family

I want to work four days per week

Make sure these are phrased in a positive way as you will achieve what you focus on. Write "<u>I want </u>to work four days a week", NOT "<u>I don't want</u> to work five days a week". In the first sentence the main emphasis is on four days. In the second sentence, it is on five.

**It is important to emphasize what you are aiming for, not what you want to avoid.**

On reflection, you may find that your current workplace is not so bad after all, but that you just need a different position, or a change of pace. If this is so, think of possibilities to free up time to enrich your life and focus on developing the skills you need to progress at work.

**(W)** **Distill your answers into concise, positively worded sentences. Write down any ideas you might have at this stage about job options.**

## (2) Make a plan

You need a plan in order to make these steps happen. It is easy to continue as you always have done unless you make a written plan that lays out <u>what</u> you will do and by <u>when</u>. It could be a few lines that show your commitment or it could be a multi-page business plan. If you don't know what you are interested in yet, your plan should be to set a date and do some research before then. Then revise as you go.

Your plan can be helped even further by the goal setting activities covered in Chapter 13. Make the first step small and achievable in a short time frame, so that you start to make some progress.

**Future steps can build on what you achieved with this first step.** Make sure you add dates to your plan and review it regularly. If you miss the dates on your plan, review why you missed them, learn from whatever happened and move on. Don't obsess about missing dates, as you are likely to be a lot further on than if you had not set a date at all!

 **Write down the first few steps of your Plan. What will you achieve by what date?**

For example, when I wrote the first edition of this book, I wanted to have it published by my birthday in March. I managed it by the middle of April, so yes, I missed the goal but if I hadn't set the deadline, I might still be working on it.

## (3) Research

Research is important, as it opens your eyes to what is possible and can give you new ideas. Research is also about testing feasibility and clarifying the details of what certain jobs entail. Keep your personal list in mind at all times so that you're alert for suitable options.

This will help you answer questions like:

What could I do?

What do I need to do it?

What does the job entail?

What will I get out of it?

Does it meet my goals and priorities?

How long will it take to get to where I want to be?

Here are some research ideas:

- **Go to job websites** or sites specializing in career advice and scan them for jobs that resonate with you. You can find approximate pay scales and requirements here too.

- **Read blogs, local and national papers** as they often profile jobs in the career section.

- **Visit University career services** or local council or government funded careers offices. They often have people who can discuss possibilities with you, as well as plenty of books on careers.

- **Investigate recruitment consultancies** in the areas you are interested in.

- **Ask people what they do** and find out the details of their job. Do they enjoy it? Does it sound like it might be for you? Find out what you would need to get into that job.

**As you go through the research process, you will reach a Decision Point.**

You will find yourself drawn to something in particular and you will need to make the decision to follow up one option. For example, you decided you want to retrain to become a teacher. You will then need to narrow this down with more research or volunteer work e.g. what subject do I want to teach, what student age, what type of school?

**You may make a decision and then find out later it was the wrong path. That's OK.**

This is how we learn more about ourselves and what we want. Until you try something, how do you even know what you want? The greater risk is not to try.

**WARNING: You can spend forever researching!**

This is "analysis paralysis" and is the dangerous state of getting bogged down in too much detail and self questioning. If this is happening, you will need to force a Decision Point on yourself. Decide on one option and pursue that first. If it doesn't work out, you can try the next idea.

(W) **Where can you find information about what you are interested in?**

Complete this sentence. "I want to _____".
Update your plan with how you will research this.

## (4) Work for Free!

Working for free is different for everyone, but it basically means giving the job a trial run. It might be volunteering for a charity or taking on some work in your spare time shadowing someone who does that job. For me, it was writing this book in the evenings and at weekends whilst still doing my full-time job. Then I transitioned to four days a week so that I could grow my online business with lower risk.

> "High performers work for free. The difference between working for free because you're a loser and working for free because you're a high performer is what you get from the deal."
>
> *Penelope Trunk*

**Working for free will enable you to gain valuable experience while still earning at the same time.**

This is important, as you may have decided you want to do a particular job but then the reality is different to what you expected. Working for free means that you can give it a try in a low-risk way without giving up your day job. Many jobs have volunteer work that you could do whilst deciding whether this is the right decision for you. Or you can ask a company if you can work for free as job experience, get an apprenticeship or try shadowing someone.

If you are investigating your own business, starting it in your spare time is less risky than giving up the day job. It gives you some security if you decide not to pursue it long term.

Volunteering your time and effort gives you the opportunity to try different things without losing your earnings. You may even get a job offer from this work experience. Remember that you can try different options, and even if they don't turn into your next career, you will get closer to finding out what fits you as a person. You will have learnt a lot and hopefully enjoyed the experience. You don't know unless you try!

During this time you will reach another Decision Point: either to pursue this option, or return to the research step if this is not what you want to do.

**W** Is this what I want to do or is there something else that fits me better? What did I enjoy about the experience? What did I not enjoy?

If you are returning to the research step, make sure you think about the reasons you are not continuing down that path and add them to your list. This will help you to keep refining your short list of key requirements.

If you have decided that this is your chosen path, then you can move onto the next step.

## (5) Re-train

This step is usually necessary if there are things you need to do in your desired job that you don't know how to do right now, or that you actually need proof of for employment. Chapter 3: Develop Yourself goes into this in more detail.

Examples of re-training may include:

- Full-time or part-time study to gain a Degree, Competency Certificate or a practical skill set

- Correspondence courses. Online, residential, weekend or informal courses

- Apprenticeships

- On-the-job training (which may also be achieved through volunteering/working for free)

**W** Do I need to re-train in order to change my career/role or job? How do I achieve this re-training?

Whilst you are re-training, you will be faced with other decisions and questions: what courses to take, what specialty to study, how to pay the bills in the meantime. This process will help you narrow down your field even further.

The main Decision Point you will have at the end of your re-training is, "Am I ready to break out of my job and get into this new career?" You will find you are excited about the process as you have something to aim for other than your current job – the end is in sight!

**But don't feel that this is the end of your choices.** You can still return to what you know or pull out of retraining. You can still decide it is not for you.

Here are some of my experiences with retraining.

After studying psychology at school and then writing my University thesis on the Psychology of Religion, I put it aside as a serious career option but continued to read psychology books for fun. After several of my other business ideas failed, I decided to retrain as a psychologist. I'd be able to escape consultancy for something intellectually challenging that would also help people. I went back to University and did a one year, full-time Graduate Diploma in Psychology with the aim of going into clinical practice. It was a fascinating year and I loved the study. But I also found out that the reality of being a psychologist was mainly working on depression or anxiety. Most jobs in New Zealand, where I lived at the time, were in the prison service, and it seemed that the reality didn't really fit with my dreams of the job. Once again, I returned to consulting and continued my search for what I really wanted in my work.

From 2008, I started to learn about internet marketing and making a living online. Although I haven't done an official degree course, I have spent thousands of hours as well as dollars on re-training for growing an internet business.

I also believe that learning is never wasted, as it keeps your brain alive and there are so many interesting things to learn in the world.

**It may be a risk to pursue a path that ultimately doesn't lead anywhere but the greater risk is to remain still and go nowhere.**

## (6) Break Out!

This is the point where you actually leave your old job behind and start following your new chosen career. It may be part time or it may be a big jump into full-time employment. It may be starting your own business, working from home, or moving cities. It's an exciting time but often a scary one. You will have doubts and fears but also exhilarating periods that will sustain you.

**Always remember that you have choices.**

You can repeat the process if you decide you want to do something different, or you can always return to what you know as a safety net.

I started with working four days a week at the day job in late 2007. I worked on writing and TheCreativePenn.com on the fifth day as well as weekends and evenings. I continued to work as an IT consultant to pay the bills at the same time. It wasn't until October 2011 that I finally gave up the day job in order to pursue being an author-entrepreneur full time. So the break-out can be a gradual one! You can read more about my journey in the bonus material at the end of the book.

## (7) Commitment
**Underpinning the whole process is commitment and persistence.**

This is your commitment to yourself and your long-term happiness, as well as the people who want you to be happy. It is your commitment to the process, which means you keep following your plan, even when it is hard.

Persistence is also important, as otherwise you will find reasons to give up.

I have been trying to find my ideal work situation since I started in the corporate world at aged 22. At age 36, after much experimentation, I have found my ideal job as an author-entrepreneur. But there are many years ahead of me as I navigate this new world. Thankfully, the challenges never stop.

(W) **Are you committed to this process of change? Why is it so important to you this time? What will happen if you do not go through with this? How can you keep yourself committed?**

"On the field of the self stand a knight and a dragon. You are the knight.
Resistance is the dragon.
The battle must be fought anew every day."

*Steven Pressfield, The War of Art*

# CHAPTER 13. SETTING AND ACHIEVING YOUR GOALS

*"The only thing that stands between a man and what he wants from life is often merely the will to try it and the faith to believe it is possible."*

### Richard M Devos

I hope that by now you are fired up about the changes you could make in your life. Perhaps you can see a path ahead of you that could lead you to a more fulfilling work life. The dream is critical, but in order to get there we need to set some specific goals so that the dream can become reality.

**People plan and set goals for things they love to do and want to achieve, such as holidays and leisure time, but often not for their working lives.**

You may have planned and achieved a number of things in your life, but you also may have never sat down and actually set goals about your job or how you want to earn your living.

Goal setting as a process is incredibly important, especially around career change or progression. It gives a target to aim for and a specific date to achieve it by.

**It focuses the mind and allows your 'mental filters' to adapt to new realities.** Dreaming about possible futures is important, as it gives you somewhere to aim for, but goal setting is a more practical activity that actually maps the path to achievement. The diagram below outlines the relationship between dreams and goals.

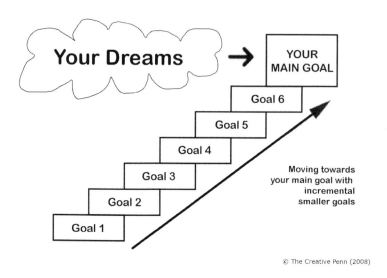

© The Creative Penn (2008)

**Dreams are important as they reveal something about what you truly want,** so don't let them disappear. I write them down in my Moleskine notebooks but sometimes it can be helpful to make a vision board, a place where you put images of what you are working toward. It might also contain key statements or quotes that resonate with you, or your goals and the steps you are taking towards them. This can be a physical board or a virtual one using a site like <u>Pinterest.com</u>.

From all the exercises you have done so far, you should be able to identify your **Main Goal**.

This is your main statement of intention and where you want to end up. To achieve this Main Goal, there will be many smaller goals you need to achieve in order to get there. Break it down into steps and you will find that once you achieve the first step, you will be able to see how to achieve the next one.

By taking it one step at a time, you will make it to your Main Goal, which is closer to achieving your dreams. Once you see how well this process works, you can set your next goals and begin again.

> (W) **What dreams do you have about the life you want or your ideal job? The Companion Workbook contains the above diagram for you to fill in your dreams. The next section will help you fill in your goals.**

There are a number of important principles to use in your goal setting process.

- **Write your Main Goal and your smaller goals in simple language** that are easy to understand and remember. Remember to word it in a positive way e.g. "I will be ..." Or "I will have ..." Or "I am ..."

- **Your goal must be measurable** so you know when you have achieved it. Your goal should also have a time limit. This gives your mind a defined limit and also means you will pay attention to how far you are getting as time passes. Again, I set the goal for the original version of this book to be finished by my birthday. I missed the goal by just under a month, but setting the boundaries enabled me to almost make it.

- **Speak your Main Goal and the specific goal** you are working on right now either out loud or in your head every day. Say it with confidence. This confidence is important, even if you don't feel it at first, because the more you get used to the words and the ideas, the more you will feel that it will happen. Writing down your goals is also critical. I now use my blog as a way to be accountable, by announcing my writing goals at the beginning of every year and then reviewing them at the end.

**Fill in your Main Goal and at least the first step on the smaller goals ladder in the Companion Workbook.**

> "Set a goal that is big enough that in the process of achieving it, you become someone worth becoming."
>
> *Jim Rohn*

## What if I change my mind?

You may fill in your Main Goal and start up the ladder of smaller goals and then find you change your mind about what you want. I have done this many times along the journey. It's clear from the **Career Change Process** that there are many Decision Points and you can change your mind at any time. This is completely normal!

Luckily, there is a time lag between setting goals and actually achieving them. You have time for change on the way. To use a skiing analogy, you can start down the slope at a diagonal and then change direction as you go. By starting, you will be heading in approximately the right direction and it's easier to turn when you're moving. You can make little changes along the way to keep yourself on the right path for what you really want.

The main problem for most people is they don't even start moving.

## Persistence

Don't stop if there are setbacks or you are discouraged.

All things worth achieving take effort and energy along the way, and this makes it more worthwhile in the end. The road will be difficult at times, but if you persevere and are persistent, you will achieve your goal. Sometimes you will feel overwhelmed and want to give up, but keep remembering the reason why you wanted to achieve your goal.

Believe that you can achieve it, that you deserve it, and remind yourself of this throughout the process. But take time off sometimes to forget about what you are aiming for. Give your mind a rest so that you can be refreshed to start again the next day.

Hold onto your desire and make this goal happen.

> "Our greatest wekness lies in giving up. The most certain way to succeed is always to try one more time."
>
> *Thomas Edison, 'failed 10,000 times before inventing the lightbulb*

(w) **What could you do to support your persistence when you start to feel discouraged? Write down why achieving your Main Goal is so important for you.**

## Take action immediately

It is important to act on your goals immediately. Set an achievable first step, then get on and achieve it. There is no need to wait now.

**Act to change your situation. You can do it!**

Be larger than your present situation and think further than where you are now. Fill the day with just a little more in order to take one step closer to your long term goals. You may have to do something you don't want to for a while, but with desire and persistence **you can change what you do in the future.**

- Be committed to improving your own life.

- Believe in yourself.

- Cut out time wasters like too much TV. In fact, ditch the TV altogether. You'll be glad you did.

- Make time for your life change and invest time and energy in yourself.

- Focus on your plan for the future.

- Keep motivating yourself – review and celebrate your successes.

- Focus on <u>why you have to achieve</u> this change.

- Take action now!

**"People often say that motivation doesn't last. Well, neither does bathing –  that's why we recommend it daily."**

*Zig Ziglar*

## Your Challenge...Your Future

> "Twenty years from now you will be more disappointed by the things you didn't do than by the ones you did. So throw off the bowlines. Sail away from the safe harbour. Catch the trade winds in your sails. Explore. Dream. Discover."
>
> *Mark Twain*

You bought this book because you don't enjoy your job, it affects the rest of your life and you wanted some help.

**You should now have plenty of ideas to implement immediately** and many more that will be useful as you move forward with your journey. If you have filled in the Companion Workbook, you will have lots of information about yourself that can help you to continue your development.

The most important thing is for you to **take responsibility right now for your life,** and take action to make it better for yourself. Whether this is a small change, or a big step into a life-changing decision, start now. Life is too short to not enjoy what you do every day.

**Make a commitment to yourself and your future.**

Make a plan of action and take steps towards the job you really want to do, towards the life you want, where you can smile and say enthusiastically, "I LOVE what I do!"

"First you jump off the cliff and then you build wings on the way down."

*Ray Bradbury*

# RESOURCES:

## Companion Workbook

This free PDF contains all the questions and diagrams from the book so you can print it and write your answers down. It is available on this page with no signup required.

www.TheCreativePenn.com/careerchange

## Recommended Reading

I am a self-help junkie and I recommend these books and resources if you want to learn more in different areas.

### Career Change

- *Escape from Cubicle Nation. From Corporate Prisoner to Thriving Entrepreneur* - Pamela Slim

- *The Four Hour Work Week. Escape 9-5, Live anywhere and join the new rich* - Timothy Ferriss

- *Career Renegade. How to make a great living doing what you love* - Jonathan Fields

- *The Way We're Working Isn't Working* - Tony Schwartz

- The *Fire Starter Sessions: A soulful and practical guide to creating success on your own terms* - Danielle La Porte

- *$100 Startup: Reinvent the way you make a living, Do what* *you love and Create a new future* - Chris Guillebeau

- *The E-Myth* - Michael Gerber

- *Linchpin: Are you indispensable?* - Seth Godin

- *Working for free article* on Penelope Trunk's blog

## Self-help/ Positive Psychology/ Life change

- *The Success Principles: How to get from where you are to where you want to be* - Jack Canfield

- *The Last Lecture* - Randy Pausch

- *The Compound Effect* - Darren Hardy

- *The Top Five Regrets of the Dying* - Bronnie Ware

- *The Happiness Project* - Gretchen Rubin

- Simon Sinek's *Start With Why* video on TED.

## Creativity

- *The Artist's Way* - Julia Cameron

- *The War of Art* - Steven Pressfield

- *A Whole New Mind: Why right-brainers will rule the future* - Daniel Pink

- *Imagine: How creativity works* - Jonah Lehrer

- *The Creative Habit: Learn it and use it for life* - Twyla Tharp

- Patricia Piccini Artworks

- Ron Mueck Sculptures

## Travel

- *There Are Other Rivers* - Alastair Humphreys

- *The power of time off* - Stefan Sagmeister TED video 17 mins

## Money

- *Rich Dad, Poor Dad* – Robert Kiyosaki
- *The Richest Man in Babylon* – George S. Classon
- *I will teach you to be rich* - Ramit Sethi
- Forbes article on Sara Blakely, billionaire with Spanx slimming undergarments

## Other Resources

- Mind Tools on Time Management. Includes information on productivity, prioritization, scheduling, concentration and focus, goal setting, motivation, and more
- *The Energy Project* - Discover a better way of working
- Many of the quotes throughout the book are from *The Challenge of Words*. This is a book full of quotes and short readings based around the key themes of the Outward Bound adventure courses.

# BONUS CASE STUDY: MICRO ENTREPRENEUR. THE CREATIVE PENN LTD

Since this book was written to help people love their jobs and potentially change career, I thought you might find it useful to understand how my business works and how I moved out of the day job to becoming a happy full-time author-entrepreneur.

First of all, figuring out the Why behind the What is critical. If you want to explore this concept further, check out Simon Sinek's *Start With Why* video on TED. You don't want to create another day job for yourself, so you need to understand your personal, lifestyle and business goals.

## My lifestyle goal:

Freedom is my ultimate aim, in terms of my time and the ability to move countries. This premise determined the following business decisions:

- The business could not be based on a physical location. There should be the ability to move anywhere with no interruption to business.

- No employees, but use of professional freelancers/contractors working virtually where necessary.

- No physical stock.

- No large fixed or variable costs. Low overheads.

- Income must be at least equivalent to earnings in business consultancy, but doing something I am passionate about. (I don't believe in the myth of the poor creative/writer in a freezing garret.)

With these aspects in mind, it suited me to start an internet business with no need for physical office space/assets/stock, as well as write books.

## My business (and personal) goals:
- To become a brand name fiction author under J.F.Penn - Ancient Mystery, Modern Thrill
- To help others write, publish and market their books through TheCreativePenn.com

## My customers:
- Fiction - lovers of thrillers, action-adventure and those people interested in religion, psychology and the supernatural.
- People who want to write books, those who have a book and want to publish or people who want to learn about online marketing for their books or small businesses.

## My business model:
- 80% scalable income. 20% time-based income.

Scalable income is when you create something once and then it can earn you money repeatedly without further effort. So it takes me a certain amount of time to write a book or create a multimedia product, but once it is created, it might sell 1 copy, or 1000, or even 1 million copies. The effort is the same but the income is scalable. Time based income is speaking or 1:1 consulting that pays once and is constrained by my physical presence.

## So how do I actually make money? Here's what I currently sell.

- **Books** I write action-adventure novels which are sold on Amazon and other ebook stores. I also write non-fiction books like this one.

- **Multimedia courses** I sell courses for writers/authors/small businesses to learn the skills they need online. I make multimedia products with video, audio and text components and then sell them from my website. The courses are reasonably priced ($20 - $199) and I sell several every day. They range from 'How To Write A Novel,' through the 'ProWriter' series, to '21 Ways To Sell More Fiction Online' and many more. Yo9u can find a complete list of courses on www.thecreativepenn.com.

- **Speaking** I have been an international professional speaker for several years now and really enjoy live presentation. I do keynotes, full day workshops and multi-day events on writing, publishing and marketing for authors and small businesses.

- **1:1 Consulting** I offer a great deal of information for free at TheCreativePenn.com as well as the premium multimedia courses, but often people need more targeted help. I offer 1:1 consulting sessions where I answer specific material prepared for the individual's situation. I call this consulting, not coaching, as people receive enough guidance to go away and proceed on their own. My aim is to empower individuals with the knowledge they need to succeed.

# How do the finances work?

It's important to consider the finances in any business, as I have learned from my mistakes in the past. An internet business where you sell your own products is a great way to make a good profit with few overheads. The high level breakdown is as follows:

## Income:

- Amazon and other ebook retailers pay by check or bank transfer every month.

- Smashwords and BookBaby, ebook distributors, pay by PayPal

- For my multimedia courses and consulting, I am paid using PayPal. When the PayPal balance reaches a certain amount, I download it to my bank account.

- For speaking, I invoice and am paid directly into my bank account.

## Expenses:

- Internet connection monthly, hosting, shopping cart, list management. Around US$150 per month.

- Home office expenses

- Professional editing and cover design for my books

- Research costs for my books including travel

## Plus:

- Ongoing investment over the last four years learning all about internet marketing, blogging, public speaking, writing and publishing from books, online courses, weekend courses, and professional memberships.

## How I changed career slowly

In Chapter 11, I shared some of the mistakes I made in my other businesses. For this move into being a full-time author-entrepreneur, I made the move slowly and with more care. Here's the timeline so you can see how the journey progressed. It's also important to note how many times I changed direction.

**1997-2011:** I worked as an IT and business consultant, specializing in SAP Financials. I started with the management consultancy firm Accenture (at that time Andersen Consulting) and then worked in boutique consultancies and freelanced for all kinds of companies, including multinationals and small start-ups. I took time out over the years to try to start various businesses but always had to go back. Consultancy paid the bills.

**July 2007-April 2008:** I wrote the first incarnation of this book entitled 'How To Enjoy Your Job.' When I sold practically no copies, I learned the hard way that I needed to know about marketing and the business side of publishing.

**April 2008-Dec 2008:** I learned about marketing from books, online programs and courses. I invested in my education. I also started several blogs. TheCreativePenn.com was started in Dec 2008 and was my third site.

**Feb 2009:** I joined Twitter and started The Creative Penn podcast as well as continuing to blog. I was making less than $100 per month online and it was still a hobby. Ebooks and self-publishing had not gone mainstream at that point but I was learning so much that I continued to blog and share what I was learning.

**Nov 2009:** I started writing 'Pentecost,' my first action-adventure thriller. I continued blogging, podcasting and producing videos on YouTube as well as connecting through Twitter and Facebook.

**Feb 2011:** 'Pentecost' was published and started to earn money from Amazon, plus I had a couple of multimedia courses selling. I was making US$500 - $1000 per month online and I could see the potential for making a full-time income. I started to write my second novel, 'Prophecy' and create more courses in order to extend the earning potential.

**Oct 2011:** I gave up IT consulting and moved into being a full-time author-entrepreneur.

**Feb 2012:** I hit my first monthly income target.

Basically, it took me four years to move careers with little risk along the way, as I built my business part-time while paying the bills with my day job. I also saved up six months income as a buffer for the move to author-entrepreneur, with the knowledge that the savings would pay the rent and bills if necessary. We also downsized our life from a four bedroom house to a one bedroom flat, as well as selling the car. So we made lifestyle changes to allow the career change. I can say it has definitely been worth it!

**You could write a profile like this for your future life and job – what does it look like?**

# DO YOU WANT TO WRITE A BOOK?

I do believe that the book you write can change your life. Whether or not you want to pursue publication, it's an amazingly rewarding thing to do. I love to help people make this dream a reality.

If you're interested in writing a book, you can find lots of information at TheCreativePenn.com, where I help people write, publish and sell their books.

Free information includes key articles, audios and videos:

- Writing

- Publishing

- Book marketing

- The Creative Penn podcast
  Over 60 hours of free audio interviews with authors, editors, marketers and entrepreneurs.

You can also join the newsletter and download the free *Author 2.0 Blueprint: Using web 2.0* tools to write, publish and sell your book here:

www.thecreativepenn.com/resources/

# ABOUT JOANNA PENN

Joanna Penn worked for 13 years as an international business consultant but is now a full-time author-entrepreneur. She is the author of *Pentecost* and *Prophecy*, in the ARKANE series of action-adventure thrillers, as well as non-fiction books.

Joanna has a Master's degree in Theology from the University of Oxford, Mansfield College and a Graduate Diploma in Psychology from the University of Auckland, New Zealand. She lives in London, England, but spent 11 years in Australia and New Zealand.

Joanna is a PADI Divemaster and enjoys traveling as often as possible. She is obsessed with religion and psychology and loves to read, drink pinot noir and soak up European culture through art, architecture and food.

Joanna's business and blog www.TheCreativePenn.com help people write, publish and market their books through articles, audio, video and online products as well as live workshops.

Joanna is available internationally for speaking events aimed at writers, authors and entrepreneurs/small businesses. You can find more information at www.thecreativepenn.com/speaking/

## Connect with Joanna online

(e) joanna@TheCreativePenn.com

(w) www.TheCreativePenn.com

(t) http://twitter.com/thecreativepenn

(f) http://www.facebook.com/TheCreativePenn

Joanna's fiction writing site – Ancient Mystery, Modern Thrill:

www.JFPenn.com

(f) http://www.facebook.com/JFPennAuthor

# ACKNOWLEDGEMENTS

Thanks to Jonathan, for your unfailing support and patience through the creation of this book. Thanks for putting up with my grumpy-stompy-ness, for doing my diagrams, for your proof reading and for bringing me flowers.

Thanks always to my Mum, Jacqueline Penn, who has always been my greatest fan and continues to show me how much you can pack into a month! Thanks for the brilliant editing, your support and your belief in me.

Thanks to my original proof reading friends: Karen Thomas, Harj Chand, Anna-Marie Fielding and Denzil Gill. I appreciate your willingness to be guinea-pigs and your honesty!

A huge thank you to Heidi Uytendaal, who believed in my ability enough to let me work 4 days a week and make this new life a reality. And thanks to Hervais Maurel, whose trust and gratitude made him the best person to work for. These two people are stars in a corporate world where few great managers exist.

Thanks to Liz Broomfield, from LibroEditing, who did the final edits and proof read.

Thanks to Derek Murphy from Creativindie who did the cover. Thanks to Dean Fetzer at Gunboss.com for the great interior formatting.

Thanks to my readers at TheCreativePenn.com who have seen my transition in the last 3.5 years from tentative first creative steps to full-time author-entrepreneur. You make my new working life fantastic every day!

# REFERENCES FROM ORIGINAL 2008 EDITION

## Quotes

Quotes throughout the book are generally from "The Challenge of Words" from Outward Bound New Zealand.

This is a little book full of quotes and short readings based around the key themes of the Outward Bound adventure courses. This includes Adventure, Dreams and Goals, Happiness, Self-acceptance, Integrity, Nature, Responsibility and Self discovery. I went on Outward Bound at aged 15 and again at aged 30. Both were life-changing experiences and I highly recommend the courses to everyone wanting to get a kick up the butt!

## MIT free online courses

http://ocw.mit.edu/OcwWeb/web/home/home/index.htm

## Books

Beatty, R.H. (2003). The Resume Kit 5th Edition

Bowe, J., Bowe.M., & Streeter, S. (Ed) (2000) Gig: Americans talk about their jobs, Three Rivers Press; New York

Byrne, R. (2006). The Secret.

Caltabiano, M.L & Sarafino, E.P. (2002) Health Psychology: Biopsychosocial interactions

Cameron, J. (1992). The Artist's Way

Canfield, J. (2006). The Success Principles.

Carnegie, D. (1970). How to Enjoy Your Life and Your Job

Carr, A. (2004). Positive Psychology: The Science of Happiness and Human Strengths

Clason, G.S. (1988). The Richest Man in Babylon

Dante, The Divine Comedy

De Botton, A. (2005). Status Anxiety

De Martini, J. (2004). How to make a hell of a profit and still get in to heaven

Frankl, V. (1985). Mans's Search for Meaning.

Gini, A.(2001) My Job, My Self: Work and the Creation of the Modern Individual

Hall, D. (1995). Jump Start Your Brain

Hill, N. (2004). Think and Grow Rich

Kelley, T., &Littman, J. (2001) The Art of Innovation: Lessons in creativity from IDEO, America's leading design firm

Kiyosaki, R. (2000). Rich Dad, Poor Dad: What the rich teach their kids about money – that the poor and middle class do not!

Kiyosaki, R., & Trump, D. and Donald Trump (2006). Why we want you to be rich: Two Men, One Message.

Macnab, F. (1998). Work: what it does for us, what we do for it

Magsamen, S. (2006). Living Artfully.

Moore, T. (1992). Care of the Soul: A guide for cultivating depth and sacredness in everyday life.

Osbon, D.K. (1995). Reflections on the Art of Living: A Joseph Campbell Companion

Penn, M.J. (2007). Microtrends: The Small Forces Behind Today's Big Changes

Peters, T. (1999) The Circle of Innovation

Pink, D. (2005) A Whole New Mind

Puder-York, M. (2006). The Office Survival Guide: Surefire techniques for dealing with challenging people and situations.

Robbins, A. (2001). Awaken the Giant Within.

Seligman, M. (1998). Learned helplessness: How to change your mind and your life

Vise, D.A. (2005). The Google Story

Whyte, D. (1996). The Heart Aroused: Poetry and the Preservation of the Soul in Corporate America.

Zikman, S. (1999). The Power of Travel: A Passport to Adventure, Discovery, and Growth

## Articles

Links to the articles referenced in this book are availalble here:

www.TheCreativePenn.com/LoveJobReferences

Please note: some of these links may be obsolete as the book was written in 2007-2008.

17888805R00094

Made in the USA
Charleston, SC
05 March 2013